Fashion, Style, and Image Consulting

By Gillian Armour AICI CIP

Revised and Updated 2018
10 9 8 7 6 5 4 3 2 1

Copyright ©2018 GILLIAN ARMOUR
All rights reserved.

ISBN 978-1502327611

Printed in the United States of America.
Set in Calibri.

Images used with permission: Microsoft, Gillian Armour, iStockPhoto, and Image Works.

Without limiting the rights under copyright reserved above, no part of this publication may be reproduced, stored in or introduced into a retrieval system, or transmitted, in any form, or by any means (electronic, mechanical, photocopying, recording or otherwise), without the prior written permission of both the copyright owner and the publisher of this book.

Note:
The scanning, uploading, and distribution of this book via the Internet or via any other means without the permission of the publisher is illegal and punishable by law. Please purchase only authorized electronic editions, and do not participate in or encourage electronic piracy of copyrighted materials. Your support of the author's rights is appreciated.

TEXTBOOK CONTENTS

ABOUT CONSULTING   5

THE 1,2,3 STEP CONSULTATION   31

Meet and Measure   33
Curate and Shop   47
Style and Polish   85

COURSE REGISTER   127

ABOUT

Stylist or Image Consultant? Let us explore.

Fashion stylists are commonly employed to style fashion shows, photo shoots, and sets for stage and film as well as parties or other events. Fashion stylists can be hired to style individual people, whether they are celebrities who need to project a certain image for their livelihood, or private people who want help figuring out their own most flattering clothes, makeup, and hairstyles.

Not surprisingly, a successful stylist must possess a strong visual sense. It helps to have a background in design: art, fashion, interior, or stage. Moreover, you absolutely must have an aptitude for color. If you have not studied color theory, the color wheel, or how color works, you will need to do so.

Having a career as a fashion stylist means, understandably, that you will need to know about fashion – including being familiar with some key reference points involving fashion history, fashion design, and the business of fashion.

Successful stylists must be able to instinctively assess their client's silhouette, proportion, body shape and body type and know how to coordinate specific looks that flatter.

As a stylist, you will likely be working on a freelance basis with other professionals such as photographers, editors, store owners, designers, clothing and accessory vendors, celebrities and personal clients. You will need to be knowledgeable about managing the project at hand. Therefore, in addition to having the artistic and the stylistic skills, you need to have some business, planning, and research experience.

You will be working with the media, so you will be expected to be well-versed in visual images and visual references. You will also likely be working in some aspect of the entertainment business – whether you are styling industry types who need to look good for presentations related to the television or film business or styling actual on-air celebrities or spokespeople.

The business of fashion styling is growing in leaps and bounds. Unfortunately, there are many stylists out there who are getting the glory with very little experience under their belt. It is critically important to be a professional, to represent the image industry so certification is crucial to your success.

Above all, as a stylist, you will need to understand that it is not about you. Your job as a stylist is to make your client look fantastic. You are in the background. Far too often I have seen celebrity stylists advance their own agenda and quickly fizzle in their businesses. You never want to overshadow your client. As a stylist, your strengths will lie in what you know, how well you do your work, and how great you make your client look. That will make your business! Do not forget word of mouth will increase the work that you do. Being professional at all times will get you more work with other professionals who respect and admire what you do.

With this book you will learn how to formulate a plan of action before approaching clients and presenting your projects. You will also learn how to create your own personal portfolio, which will act as a visual resumè when you go out to approach clients for work. You will become familiar with the core principles of consulting and styling and learn all the responsibilities of a professional stylist.

IMAGE CONSULTING

Image consulting (also known today as impression management, clothing consulting, fashion stylist or image coach, etc.) has boomed in the past 10 - 15 years becoming a true profession, well respected in the wider fashion world. Many women have been drawn to its fashion and style aspects, appreciating the profession's emphasis on personal appearance, having seen in their own lives the power of a good first impression.

On the down side, some people are attracted to the profession because it is easy to enter. One does not need college degrees or specialized training (though that certainly helps). They assume all that's needed to enter the image consulting field is some knowledge of dressing, hair, makeup and shopping, things they do every day. In fact, as we shall see, to be a successful image consultant involves knowledge of much more than these basic 'feminine' skills.

Today image consultants can be found around the world. While anyone with, or without, experience can hang out a shingle saying they are in business, it is the professionally certified who get the most clients, command the highest fees, have the highest respect of their peers (and of themselves) and, in my opinion, best serve their clients and the fashion industry.

In recent years fashion stylists have seen their success quotient rising as many gain fame working with celebrity clients. Stylists such as Philip Block, Rachel Zoe, Jessica Paster and Robert Verdi have spawned books, television shows and fan clubs about themselves! Celebrity stylists are the most recognizable by virtue of their proximity to famous clients but there are hundreds of highly talented stylists working silently away at creating visual beauty in many fields.

Contemporary stylists find success as writers and bloggers. Many stylists have created a niche of their own by blogging the latest fashion, photographing fashion influencers and reporting on key trends via their sites.

SKILLS AND TALENTS

We are not all born with set talents that propel us into highly successful careers as stylists. Most of us have to find and nurture various talents as we grow. We may have an intense interest in fashion, art, design and film as teenagers, but as adults those interests may wane when the reality of 'getting a job' comes along.

If you feel you have 'it', do not let others convince you that you don't have what it takes! Everyone with a passion for something they want to do has what it takes. There will be people in the fashion industry who may try to discourage your journey - either because they don't want the competition or because they feel inferior. Had I listened to the doubters, I would not be writing this!

Other skills you will need include enthusiasm, the ability to organize, the ability to work as part of a team, a good eye for color, an innate sense of fashion and style, the ability to reference historical styles, initiative, and an outrageous feel for creativity. Possessing a flair for coordinating fashion items and having a good sense of how to pose models for photos helps enormously. And did I mention enthusiasm?

INTERNING, APPRENTICING and VOLUNTEERING

The best way to become a successful stylist is to absorb your being into any fashion related job you can find - even if pays nothing or very little. The experience of working in and being exposed to the business is what counts. Volunteer for photographers, use your friends for makeovers, color collage an art piece or get a summer internship in a gallery or at a magazine.

There are so many jobs that can lead you into styling. Well-known celebrity stylist Rachel Zoe's path was through modeling. She posed a few times and quickly found her calling behind the camera, styling others for shoots. Other stylists such as Kendall Farr (**The Pocket Stylist**) have come to styling via editorial positions with fashion magazines.

Retail is another path. If you are just starting out in a fashion career, consider taking an entry-level job with a retailer (both large and small). Many retailers need display help, sometimes seasonally and sometimes for special events. Check with your local retailers to see what options there are for work that interests you.

Photographers are always on the lookout for assistants. When you assist a photographer, you get behind the scenes experience at photo shoots. You learn such skills as lighting techniques, use of props, scene creation, hair and makeup, computer monitor photo editing and review, and much more. It's helpful as well to study and practice photographing and styling mock shoots on your own.

Working for fashion designers introduces you to the world of fit, fabric, cloth, color, shape, silhouette and detail. Practical skills such as cataloging, coordinating, line sheet compilation and sample production are just a few of the many stylist related jobs at the design level. Other intern or volunteer jobs for the potential stylist can include the following.

Hair styling - volunteer your time to help with a hair show. Salons are always in need of an extra pair of hands.

Makeup artist - department stores often need help with product demonstrations. Interning as a product demo artist gets you connected with potential clients as well.

Freelance visual merchandising - boutiques and department stores hire seasonal help for window display and visual events. One summer in high school I volunteered at the local department store to help decorate their windows for Christmas. They called me the following Valentine's Day to help out again.

Freelance writing - find local events you can write about and offer this information to local publications and websites.

Blogging or e-reporting - this is an automatic career decision. Every stylist has to have a blog.

Fashion show production - most fashion designers and fashion show producers need more help than they can ever get. This is a shoo-in if you want to help out. One word of caution, always get permission from the designer or the producer before you start work. Just because your friend says it's ok, doesn't make it so.

Fashion show dresser - because fashion shows are usually big productions there are many jobs that could utilize your talents. Charity fashion shows usually have committees organized into the following:

- Show Concept and Planning Development
- Fashion Show Production
- Donation Coordination
- Backstage Management and Dressers
- Styling and Alterations
- Commentators

Trunk show assistant - trunk shows usually take place in departments stores and boutiques. They are an opportunity for a designer to network with existing and potential clients. Trunk shows are sometimes accompanied by a fashion show and are coordinated by staff in the stores. Contact local jewelry or fashion designers.

Storyboard artist - fashion storyboards allow you to tell a story or explain a theme. They are often paired with a "mood board", a collection of influences such as photographs, fabric colors, and things from nature, evocative of that story's mood. When you create one of these boards for the designer be sure to keep a copy for your portfolio.

Sewing - and this includes alterations as well. While volunteer or intern seamstress jobs may seem petty or menial, for a stylist they are in fact very important basic skills. Again, a good choice for sewing work would be a fashion designer, a local tailor, custom clothier, or dry-cleaning establishment.

Volunteering - to help at local fashion charity events puts you into the networking loop with potential clients. Check out local non-profit event listings in your area on the Internet or in the newspaper to see what is happening. Make sure that the events you volunteer for are in line with your interests and career goals and can help you get connected with people who can advance those goals and/or feed those interests. And, of course, your volunteer work provides services that are of assistance to the community.

When contacting a volunteer organization tell the recruiter what you would like to do or what services you can provide. Mention your special skills; they might really be needed. The recruiter will most likely give you work or assign you to a project that makes use of your fashion skills and allows you to develop new ones.

In summary, here are a few ideas to help get you moving forward in experience:

- Get on the mailing lists of local schools (beauty and fashion) for info on their events.
- Sign up at local department stores to help assist dressing models for fashion shows.
- Contact fashion designers in your area and offer to intern.
- Be on the lookout for ads in local publications, local websites and even on bulletin boards.

EDUCATION

There are many fashion, art, design, photography and film schools ready to enroll students who show an interest in learning skills to launch careers. Choosing which one to attend can be a daunting experience. There are many factors involved when you set out to choose a school. We cannot possibly cover the broad range of options available to future stylists here BUT we can give you a few pointers to help you on your way.

First, narrow down your interests. Think about your passions and analyze the direction they have taken you. Ask yourself questions about the jobs you have had in the past and the experiences that have come your way – what did you like or not like? What did you like enough to want to pursue further?

Keep in mind that formal education is not a requirement for a successful fashion styling career. Work experience, contacts, good taste and a practiced "eye" are the most important talents you need to succeed. Combine these assets with the previously mentioned enthusiasm and reliability and the fashion world is your oyster.

In order to learn the basics about fashion, color and image, I would recommend taking small courses to round out specific experience or knowledge you are lacking. Many image consultants offer courses in these subjects. You can get a complete listing of Fashion Styling and Image Consulting courses on line at **www.aici.org**. This site is for the Association of Image Consultants International (AICI), a global organization that upholds gold-standard certifications for Image and Style professionals.

You will also want to do a fair amount of "self-education" by studying the latest fashion magazines and periodicals to educate yourself on recent style movements, current trends, updates on designers and more. The more you know about up to the minute trends in design and style, the more inventive you can be. You can use this information for the creative components of your projects.

STYLIST TIP
Be plugged in. As a stylist, you influence trends and create new, exciting looks for fashion followers so, be plugged in to current events happening around you. Know who the hot new bands are, the latest eatery to open or who is dating whom for example. All these cultural threads can lead back to the work you do to create an exciting vision for the client.

GETTING WORK

What does a fashion stylist do? In a nutshell, a fashion stylist creates an image that sends a message about a person, product or event through visual references using the media of magazines, fashion shows and television shows. Stylists also work with personal clients on a one-on-one basis, with 'celebrities' by helping to craft their image or with fashion designers to style editorially and stylists can find challenging jobs and projects in a number of ways.

Getting styling jobs within a specific industry takes effort, enthusiasm, persistence, networking and just plain luck. You must be prepared to start somewhere, anywhere really, if you are beginning your career in fashion styling.

Often stylists get jobs assisting fashion designers, costumers, photographers, visual merchandisers or other stylists, including hair and makeup artists. Be sure to focus in on the jobs that are in the fashion and apparel industries. There are various industries that use stylists – interior design, art galleries, jewelers, food and beverage, floral, etc.; however, this book focuses on the fashion industry only.

The most valuable aspect of being a fashion stylist is having actual hands-on work experience. When you work with department stores, galleries, hair salons or photographers, you are also gaining contacts to add to your networking and experience databases. You never know when you will need to call on these contacts and resources for help - so never burn your bridges.

Work experience also allows you to begin your portfolio creation. Not only will you have to update your résumé constantly, but your portfolio should include examples with photos of your recent work. Styling is a visual medium and you will want to have visual record of the projects you have successfully completed. Be sure to include a list of references with contact information in your portfolio.

FREELANCERS

Many stylists are freelancing and have their own businesses. This can be risky in many ways, because you never know if there will be money flowing in or not and, unless you have money saved, you might struggle between jobs. However, as a freelancer, you can set your own hours, pick the clients you want to work with (as opposed to having them assigned) and have more creative leeway with the projects and clients you take on. Freelancing is a great way to build your work portfolio and to increase your network of clients.

FREELANCE STYLING OPPORTUNITIES

- On-call stylist for hotels, event planners, wedding planners
- Consulting for makeup artists
- Assisting photographers
- Stylist for celebrities, politicians, local newscasters
- Teaching at a modeling school, classes on style and fashion for teens
- Visual merchandising for pop-up stores
- Styling for retail shops (jewelers, boutiques etc.)
- Assisting with trunk shows for major designers and department stores
- Organizing trunk shows for smaller designers, jewelers and artists
- Fashion designer showrooms (set up collections, line sheets and displays)
- Writing for local publications, your own blog, your own website
- Assisting in a PR office
- Casting models for events
- Creating props and scenery for special events

MEDIA (MAGAZINES AND OTHER PUBLICATIONS INCLUDING ONLINE BLOGS)

Editorial stylists work closely with the editors of magazines. These could be fashion, art or design editors writing or editing pieces for a magazine or newspaper. Most major fashion magazines have a steady roster of stylists they use repeatedly.

If you are hired by a media outlet to style for their stories, you will need to establish your fees in advance. You will also need to know the protocol for getting the right merchandise to showcase. Editors sometimes pull from designers, and may send you out to collect the merchandise, though more commonly, designers will send in samples for the editors to feature.

A great way to establish yourself as an expert is to start your own website or blog. Become a fashion stylist blogger – think of Scott Schulman of the *Sartorialist*. He started taking photos of people he saw on the street who styled their clothing in fascinating ways. His blog is now a reference resource for fashionistas in need of inspiration and he was recently offered his own reality TV show! As a rule of thumb any successful stylist should have at least one blog as part of their portfolio. It shows others your talents and allows them to interact with you as a stylist/writer.

PHOTOGRAPHERS

For a stylist, working on a photo set/shoot is an adrenaline rush bar none. There is constant movement, constant creation and invention, reinvention and discarding of ideas and thoughts.

Working with photographers can give you a great education in lighting, color, set decoration, artistic collaboration and image making. Some of the responsibilities of the job require booking models for the shoot, sizing them and getting their outfits coordinated, model sheet review (models size, clothes line up, shoes and accessory listing), pulling clothing, hiring hair and makeup teams, accessorizing the outfits and reviewing final images on computer.

Many photographers partner exclusively with stylists and build long-term relationships that last through many campaigns. Because the two have to work so closely to create the vision for the client, the elements of trust, respect and mutual enthusiasm for the project can be sustained when the relationship is firm.

Great stylists make it a point to know the models on the scene, so they can refer to them when a photographer needs a particular look. Stylists are crucial when it comes to casting, because they work with many models and they know the shapes and faces to carry the look of the designs and makeup. Stylists can make real the often abstract ideas that clients put forth for their vision. They also have a knack for the overall composition of the photographic image – how the model moves, holds her posture, displays the garment or translates the emotion needed.

Photographers typically develop their core teams of stylists, makeup, assistants and lighting experts, so if you want repeat work, do great work with the photographer (and do not forget the fundamentals: enthusiasm and reliability). On many shoots, this team of professionals also contributes to the final editing of the images.

FASHION DESIGNERS

Stylists for designers are often employed to interpret a designer's vision for the clothing line. Whether that interpretation evolves through fashion shows, online blogs, newsletters or other media format, it is up to the stylist to craft the visual message based on the designer's specifications. Often design assistants take up this mantle of responsibility, but just as often freelance stylists are hired for a fresh take (a new 'eye') on the designer's vision.

Designer stylists also help compile and edit Look Books (a photographic record of the seasonal lines for sale) and create Line Sheets (detailed information about the seasonal lines/ products for sale such as style, style control unit (sku) and price points).

Stylists also help to coordinate the design, setup, facilitation and breakdown of various booth displays for market shows, events, photo shoots and editorial sessions.

Stylists are often hired to style a photo shoot for a designer. This is usually seasonal, and shoots involve significant effort and coordination. Models have to be booked, accessories coordinated, outfits styled and pressed and shoes ready to complete the look. Makeup and hair stories must match the mood of the clothing and the story. It is the job of the stylist to tie the whole scene together, to hold the vision and to deliver it all for the designer.

ENTERTAINMENT INDUSTRY

There are many job opportunities for stylists in the entertainment industry. Storyboard preparation and presentation, wardrobing, script analysis, and costume illustration for film and television are just a few of the jobs that require the skills of a stylist.

When you work for the entertainment industry, your resume, your portfolio and your cadre of clients will fill fast. If you are talented, the word will spread rapidly and you will get a lot of work.

You may have to start at the very bottom of this world and work up the ladder to greater success. Volunteer to be an intern to work on sets if you can. Find the website of the local film commission and contact their offices for jobs. Remember, if you are starting from the bottom, any job they can offer you should take.

Once you have your foot in the door, be enthusiastic, be positive, be reliable and be a team player. People skills are crucial for success in film and television because you will be working with large egos and demanding employers. Do not damage your reputation or burn your bridges, because in this circle, word travels fast.

When working with celebrities in their work environment, always be professional. On-set work is different from the individual styling work you do with famous clients. Celebrity stylists working on set are usually there in the capacity of wardrobing.

Be on the lookout for styling jobs that give you the work experiences you need to fill in your portfolio; costume and wardrobe organization, set design assistant, makeup artist assistant to name a few. I know stylists who have had great success approaching local celebrities in their town. Newscasters, politicians and socialites always need a stylist's assistance. Bonus – working with them gives you exposure and credibility! Do not be shy about approaching them. Sometimes you must work through their publicists to get to them but that is just a formality.

STORYBOARD PREPARATION AND PRESENTATION

Stylists create storyboards for a better understanding of script/story analysis and to interpret the script/story in a visual manner. An understanding and ability to translate plot, character, conflict, crisis and climax on the boards is the skill-based work done here. Stylists use visual tools and techniques to storyboard scenes in a way that presents the story in the best, most interesting and clearest way possible.

WARDROBING

Wardrobing means to manage the wardrobe requirements of a project, whether it is film, television, stage or theatre. The wardrobe stylist works with the costume designer, the wardrobe manager, the production crew and others.

It is important to know the hierarchy and the job description before you begin, so always check with the set, stage and costume designers for their input before you start work on the project.

You will be asked to supply costumes from wardrobe that fit a particular scene or storyline, so it is important you know the inventory. Most costume departments keep very careful records not just about their inventory, but about when certain styles were worn, by whom and for what purpose.

In general, the wardrobist is supplied with directives for fashion coordination from the wardrobe manager or the head costumer. Depending on the budget you may also be supplied with a story line or design brief from the costumer. The design brief can include photographs of ideas, fabric swatches, color palettes, notes about the characters, notes about the scenes, the location story and other pertinent details that will help the costumer create the outfits and costumes the actors wear to represent their characters.

RETAILERS

Retailers offer some of the best initial jobs for future stylists. The list is endless, but the two areas of specialization include marketing and merchandising. Within the retail marketing division, jobs in visual display and visual merchandising require a good eye, color sense, design and fashion sense and creativity.

Effective visual merchandising requires you to know about design composition for creating successful displays. You will need to know about color and color planning for the retail selling floor. Some days will be spent creating props, selecting proper lighting and working with store fixtures. Other days will be filled with creating sets and stories within the departments using mannequins, flowers, signage and props.

Visual merchandisers are also called upon to coordinate new fashion collections on the sales floor and assist with fashion show setup (stage, lighting, backstage and props). On occasion, large promotions such as trunk shows by visiting designers will engage your visual skills.

As with the entertainment industry, getting a foot in the door of retailing can take you far. Many working stylists began their careers on the floors of boutiques and department stores around the world (myself included).

Additional Opportunities in Retail for Fashion Stylists:

Merchandise Planner - partners with buyers to implement and manage merchandise assortments in all stores.

Merchandise Coordinator - participates in selecting product from the store ordering system that will satisfy customers' demand, fill the planned sales floor space, and support the merchandise presentation and inventory content objectives for the store.
Trunk Show Assistant - fashion designers who make personal appearances in stores, galleries or at events will bring special merchandise and one-of a-kinds with them, and they often need assistants. The term "trunk show" refers to the old way traveling salespeople would sell their goods – from a trunk!

Display Assistant - helps the display director with the visual images created throughout the store. Window displays, merchandising new clothing and creating shadow box vignettes are all part of a display assistants job.

Buying Office Assistant - an assistant buyer (whether junior or senior) focuses on computer and online tracking, re-ordering, merchandise planning and promotional aspects. Some visual merchandising skills are needed.

Special Events Coordinator - works under the umbrella of the marketing and PR departments of retailers. Their responsibilities include researching, designing, planning, coordinating, and evaluating special and promotional events.

Holiday Display Crew - the pixies of the season, these magic stylists transform entire stores overnight. Working off planned themes, sketches and story boards, the display team works to highlight seasonal merchandise. A strong visual and color sense is required!

Staff Fashion Meetings - many department stores hold in-house meetings to review trends, bestsellers and other newsworthy subjects with store personnel. Coordinating and planning these meetings requires a stylist to produce slide shows, story boards, newsletters and video. Usually, when buyers return from their overseas buying trips, visual recaps of highlighted trends will be previewed for staff.

Advertising Presentations - In some buying, marketing and planning offices, stylists are recruited to create story boards, visual presentations and slides or videos relating to advertising campaigns planned for the season ahead.

Grid Designs and Planner - these fashion professionals manage how to display the new assortments of merchandise from a particular line or designer.

There are many variations on retail selling outlets that can be excellent learning environments for budding stylists. These include the following: specialty shops, which specialize in designer and exclusive offerings; luxury designer stores such as Neiman Marcus, Cartier, and Gucci; apparel chains such as The Gap, The Limited, Forever 21; and small neighborhood boutiques.

Malls often hire stylists to coordinate the various fashion events held there. Mall management offices typically have a merchandising staff to keep the image of the mall consistent amongst the diverse shops and department stores.

THE BEAUTY INDUSTRY

There are also job options available in the beauty industry, primarily styling for shows, commercials, and special events. This is a great way for you to expand your skills, to get leads for jobs and to build your portfolio. I have mentioned a few already (hair salons, cosmetic lines, beauty schools) that are often on the lookout for seasonal help. Check with your local businesses for any job openings, volunteer, intern or otherwise.

Hair styling – the beauty industry is a hot bed of talent and getting your feet in the door is easiest through hair and beauty salons. Cosmetology schools offer curriculum in hair styling, makeup, salon ownership, and product representation. Beauty school graduates often move into a more advanced position, such as salon owner, professional salon consultant, make-up artist for television & movies, hair designer for magazine fashion models, cosmetic beauty advisor, or instructor.

Makeup Artist – once you are active in your career as a makeup artist your portfolio can grow to include projects with photographers, stylists, fashion show producers, film and theatre productions, department stores, direct sales reps (product demos) and editors for magazines, newspapers etc.

There are many other options available to you in the beauty industry such as styling for shows, commercials, special events. This is a great way for you to expand your skills, to get leads for jobs and to build your portfolio.

PERSONAL CLIENTS

When you are working as a professional fashion stylist you are a professional first and a stylist second. Your responsibilities will run the gamut, from fetching coffee for a sleepy actress to dressing famous people for big events. No matter what, always maintain your professionalism.

For some women, getting dressed is just a chore. For others, it is the act of creating a work of art. Most of your clients fall between these two extremes and just want to know how to look and feel great in what they wear.

 As a stylist, it is your job to be creative when working with clients on their appearance. Stylists differ from image consultants in that they are more intent on forming creative personal images for their clients. Image consultants create set images (classic, romantic, businesslike, dramatic). A stylist "pops" the images but avoids (hopefully) over-the-top looks.

Fashion stylists find their own mix of style, color, line and silhouette. Experience has taught them that cookie cutter fashion looks belong in the realm of the fashion beginner. Clients who hire stylists are looking for edgy and individual looks and, since they often do not know how to interpret what they see on the runway to make it their own, they copy or buy strictly label. Neither look is unique. It is the job of the stylist to interpret the client's needs, balance those needs with what is in fashion, use the "runway", and labels creatively and uniquely for the client, and, finally, make sure it fits and it flatters.

THE CLIENT RELATIONSHIP

Let us now explore the basics of developing client relationships. Before you start working with clients, you should explicitly agree to maintain a proper business relationship with them. Always keep it professional and do not confuse your business relationship with a possible personal one.

In general, clients do not want a personal relationship with a stylist. They are hiring you; it is a job. So even if you are being told that your work is fantastic, and they keep hiring you, remember, this is a professional relationship and nothing more, or less. Do not take it personally if they decide to hire someone else for the next job, even if they have used you forever. Sometimes the fashion styling business can be fickle, and clients have the right to decide who, when and why they want to work with someone.

Of course, you need to be networking to generate business and on occasion will be at cocktail parties, art openings or other events where you may run into your clients. This is part of the job and is necessary for your business to grow. I have frequently been invited to socialize with clients, but I always politely turn them down. I do not want to blend the professional with a personal relationship.

KNOW THE CLIENT'S PERSONALITY, TASTES & NEEDS

I always start each new relationship with a client BEFORE I even meet them. My résumé is my website and it tells most prospective clients many things; my site is me. And yours should be too. Your website is your introduction to clients, so it needs to reflect clearly and creatively who you are as a professional. Once you have met your client, be it over the phone or in person, you can begin to assess their needs, so be prepared and start asking questions. Included in this book is a sample initial 'interview' that you can tailor for first meetings with your clients.

When you meet your client for the first time in person, your own image should be impeccable. After all, your visual appearance should tell your client exactly what you want her to know about you. Present a professional image, dress smart and comfortable, be your expressive best, but do not dress to intimidate.

Remember that your interactions with clients should always be confidential (see credo in the Introduction). It would be both unwise and unprofessional to gossip or share the confidences of your client with others.

Begin your sessions with clients by focusing on the task at hand – them. They may be hiring you to polish their image, to help them land a job or to get them a date! But most of the time your personal clients will want one thing only, to look and feel great with your help. During the initial interview with your client use the sample interview forms in Chapter 6; then discuss each of these points in order to find out who your client really is:

a) Their lifestyle – leisure activities, sports, travel, social life, etc.

b) What they do for fun – dinner out, gallery walks, museum tours…

c) Why do they think they need your help?

d) When will they need your help?

e) What upcoming appearances, events, jobs, and social occasions will they need you for? Use your calendar and start taking note of the dates they give you.

f) List their favorite clothing designers.

g) Ask about personal tastes, likes & dislikes about fashion, art, style.

h) Take measurements (if applicable to the project) and define body shape. Use forms supplied in Chapter 6.

i) Process wardrobe lists and worksheets (Chapter 9).

j) Make a shopping list.

Only when you have completed your initial interview with your client, can you move on to the second part of the client interview process. This may take a while, so you might want to schedule a second session, which is how it is referred to on the next page.

BRING OUT OR CLARIFY THEIR VISION

Once you know who your client really is, the next step is to get clear (get on the same page, if you will) about the vision they have because it is your job to realize that vision. Frequently your clients will not be able to articulate a clear vision to you. Therefore, it is also your job to elicit information from them that requires asking questions, many questions. Your goal is to get the best picture of their vision as possible.

Below are a few questions I will ask clients to help get them focused. As you gain experience in this process you will start to develop your own way of getting clients to formulate and articulate their visions.

a) "Tell me how you see yourself at the end of our work together."

b) "What is your vision for yourself (for the project)?"

c) "What kind of research do we need to do?"

d) "What kind of background information can you give me that will help me create a successful look, project and end result?"

e) "If you had to pull references, what would they be? Fashion history, fashion designers, celebrity looks?"

f) "Give me some personal history that will help me understand who you are as a person."

g) Brainstorm session – you can draw pictures with client of ideas they have, do a collage of cutouts from magazines, start a story board with them.

Based on all the information you gather, tell them what you think the picture of them (or the picture of the project) is starting to look like. Do not give them all the details yet but always pay attention to the client's feedback. You will flesh out ideas later, in your own time, and will use your own method of storyboarding, scrap booking or look-books.

©Fashion Style and Image Consulting

STYLIST TIP
No matter whom your client is, personal or professional; they deserve your undivided attention during the consultation. Beware of distractions such as cell phones or overly friendly pets. Focus on your client only.

DISCOVER AND DETAIL THEIR BUDGET

The ideal time to discuss costs and budgets with clients is during one of the first two interviews – in fact, it is a must. Most clients have a good idea about how much money they want to spend. Sometimes they are way off and need to be gently brought back to reality. Because financial matters are sensitive, you must always, always write the details down. Even before you work up a formal budget presentation for the client you will be making notes of what you discussed when it came to money.

Whether your client is an individual or a business, financial details are important so clear financial communications that are always reduced to written agreements, should be at the top of your list. Successful budget controls, and client relations, depend on it. Your client will want to have an open and honest relationship with you about their budgetary concerns, limitations and abilities.

I usually start the financial conversation by asking clients what their projected expenditure/ budget is. I use these questions to get the ball rolling:

- Have they thought about the details of the project and the costs involved in accomplishing their vision?

- How much time do they expect to spend to get the project completed?

- Do they want full service packages (full image makeover, shopping trips and spa service) or just menu items (such as color analysis, body shape and measurements)?

- Explain your fees for various services. Decide if the project will be billed per hour or flat rate and create written agreements.

PERSONAL SHOPPING GUIDELINES

Once you have worked out the "why" and "how" of her needs, and agreed on the overall budget, if 'personal shopping' is part of the package, a shopping budget is needed. It is very important as a stylist to establish a budget BEFORE you shop. Never assume the amount of money she has to work with. You are not being realistic if you think that not doing a budget is OK with your clients. Creating a budget and sticking to it are the mark of a professional fashion stylist.

Planning what to shop for is also essential, in several ways. It focuses your client while you shop, AND it saves time for both of you. The sample plan is a clothing list, but you can use a similar spreadsheet with any other category of shopping needs.

Ask her about the gaps in her wardrobe, and then fill in the boxes on your spreadsheet. Your first column might be headed "has," your second "needs," and the third column "goes with" (so you can offer her options and extend the usefulness of her wardrobe).

You also need to establish how you will be reimbursed for expenses. Never use cash; it is too hard to document. Many stylists buy product from retailers and bill to their client's accounts. Some purchase on business credit cards. Later, when the client has chosen the items to keep, you will return the remaining items to the retailer for credit.

Another option is to create an open-to-buy account with your client that is funded by them. You write (or charge) any expenses to the client and they are billed. Likewise, when you return items, the client is credited. When you establish an open-to-buy account with your client you must put such details in writing as:

- How easy is your access to funds?

- Will there be a funded limit?

- By credit card or check?

If you buy merchandise and then invoice the client, you should agree to the terms of invoicing first. For example: Will you bill the client for all expenses? An example would be: cost of item + your services (more about your fees later) + special charges (overnight shipping, alterations, etc.). The point is that you must DETAIL everything, especially financial matters, when you contract with a client.

If items are on loan (borrowed) from a retailer or designer there may be costs involved – shipping charges, cleaning, fixing etc. Who will pay for these? How are they paid for? You should also establish:

- Clients projected expenditure – have a healthy, open discussion about their budget.

- Costs to complete project – give them an estimate (or quote) in writing, being sure to specify "quote only".

- Time to complete project = remember, time is money. Again, write down an estimate or quote.

- How you can spend their money efficiently – let clients know that you are fiscally responsible, budget conscious (committed to staying within their budget) and will always review planned purchases with them.

- Whether the client prefers expense sheets or invoices for reimbursements.

If borrowing items from retailers get agreements from them and supply pull sheets.

PRESENT a COLLAGE/STORY BOARD/PITCH

Preparing a collage, a storyboard, or even a "look book" presentation is a great way to encapsulate every detail, want, and wish your client has expressed during the initial interview. Detail with visuals - do not get number, graph, or text heavy. Visual references and ideas convey your plans quicker.

I created a storyboard for a shoot I did recently. This shoot was for an article I wrote that detailed the options for tops to go with "boyfriend" jeans. I wanted to show a feminine look, classic and preppy. In order to get my ideas across to the editor before we did the shoot I collaged my storyboard and she got an immediate visual image of how the photos would hang together and play out in her publication.

DISCUSS THE CONSULTANT CREDO - this is a key part of the relationship with your clients. I typically use this with each new PERSONAL client and sometimes use a modification of it with PROFESSIONAL clients. You can tailor this to your liking. The key to this agreement is that it spells out the way you want your clients to be with you and makes it clear to them how you expect the relationship to work.

WRITE CONTRACTS - if you need legal advice, there are many reference sources on the Internet. If you can afford to pay an attorney to do simple contracts for you then do so. You have been provided with a sample contract in this book, which, with your attorney's advice, can be customized, for your business.

DECIDE PRICE - negotiate knowing what your fee is for the project. Do not negotiate without knowing all the factors involved in getting the project/ job done.

IMPLEMENT THE PROJECT AND DELIVER - establish time lines with the client. Schedule the appointments by time, date and location. Stay in communication with the client about even the most mundane of details. It will serve your reputation as a complete professional very well.

CLOSE THE PROJECT - make sure the client is satisfied with your delivery of the project. Were things to her liking? Did you stick to the budget? Achieve the results? If you succeeded, ask for a testimonial to add to your portfolio. Most clients will be thrilled to be asked. If you intend to publish her testimonial publicly, you will need to get permission to do so.

ASK FOR MORE - if your clients love the work you do, ask them for referrals. Many will spread the word to their friends. If their transformation at your hands is jaw-dropping, her friends will run to you!

WORKING WITH CELEBRITIES

First, let us clarify a few terms: The term "celebrity stylist" has two meanings – it can either refer to someone who is a famous stylist, a "celebrity" in their own right OR refer to a stylist who styles for celebrities. For our purposes I am using the latter definition and will use the phrase "celebrity styling" as the job description for this special category of fashion styling.

As stated in the consultant's credo in the Introduction, all work you do with clients is confidential. Protecting the privacy rights of all clients, famous or not, is mandatory. Most celebrities will ask you to sign confidentiality agreements with them. It is a good idea and an excellent business practice. You can make this a standard part of your contractual agreements with all clients, not just celebrities. (Chapter 9 contains a sample).

Also remember that if you publicly try to advance your work with celebrities by mentioning their names in interviews, you risk losing them as clients. Celebrities are extremely sensitive to the prospect of others using them for personal gains (understandably... as it happens to them a lot). Do not fall into this trap. Your reputation will be damaged! Again, the world of famous people is a small one, and word travels fast. Conversely, if they love working with you, they will send many referrals your way.

Styling for celebrities takes patience and persistence. There may be occasions when you are with the client for hours on end. They are busy people and juggle many projects themselves. You have been contracted to work a project for them so stay patient and do the best you can.

Sometimes you will be called to do a photo shoot with your famous client. You may be asked to accompany her to the shoot to help with her choices of clothing. You will need to have a thorough understanding of your client's famous body, her best features, and her flaws. Know in advance, what she likes and does not like ...and how that will fit into her image.

Always ask yourself the following before you choose clothing to style: What is their image? Celebrities put a lot of effort into crafting a presentable image to the world. Their public image may not match their private one. The important point is that you are hired to help them advance their existing image - or to craft a newer, updated one. Often stylists are called in to fix a style and image problem, especially with new and young celebs who haven't had the time, or who lack the knowledge, to craft their personal style with clothing and accessories. It's up to you to get them on track. How do you do this?

One tip: Go back to the beginning of this chapter and follow the steps for client relationships. Also, help your celebrity client find her fashion direction. Work with her and ask pointed questions *and* take a lot of notes: Where does she think she is heading with her career image? What words best describe how she would like to be seen?

 Remember as a stylist you need to focus on advancing the client's image. Note as well that sometimes you might be really off with your wardrobe and styling choices, or the celeb will have an off day and you might risk negative publicity. You'll develop a tough skin soon enough. The more you work with celebs and their individual and career demands, the tougher your skin will become. You cannot take things personally. Even if the celeb takes it all out on you, blaming any bad publicity on what she wore, be professional. After all, you did the best you knew how. Such are the negative aspects of being in the public eye. However, when things go well, and your talents are noticed, and compliments given, you can feel on top of the world!

Another important point for you to keep in mind when working with this type of client, do not take advantage of either their fame or their wallet. You are a hired professional there to do a great job. You are not there to advance your own agenda, to ask for favors, to curry approval or to spend their money frivolously. Celeb's can smell a fake miles away and if you seriously want to progress in this career niche you will have to be honest, reliable, responsible, and above all professional.

Never invite yourself to any of your client's events, even if she asks you along. You are her stylist and that is all. You may feel that you are more to her… but you aren't. One moment she will think you are the greatest thing since sliced bread, and the next she may be working with your competitor. Again, do not take it personally. Celebrities have their own way of doing business, and you will quickly learn the way this game is played.

Frequently you will be asked to travel with your client. Before you do so, make contractual agreements regarding expenses and costs of such details as hotel rooms, per diem (expense allowances per day), airfare and other travel costs, including meals, car or other transportation. Always be crystal clear with the client regarding who is paying for what. If she is footing the bill, you will need a contract that gives you permission to spend when you need to. For instance, you might need to hit a designer showroom to look for a gown for an awards event your client is attending. In that case, taxi and meal expenses will factor into your job.

Be telegenic since you may be seen! Get trained in presentation skills; it is important that you represent well as an expert in your field. As part of your job, you may be asked to make personal appearances on TV and you may be sought after as a style expert and an authority on fashion. If you are not trained or coached in media skills, again, I highly recommend you consult experts who are. The last thing you want to do is tarnish your own image by being ill prepared and clumsy on camera.

Celebrities have their own PR specialists (often referred to as "publicist"). You and she/he will often be interacting with your shared client. I strongly advise you to maintain a fantastic relationship with your client's publicist. She is a valuable ally to have.

THE STYLING SESSION

When styling you have to think outside the box of generic fashion coordination. Styling is about being creative and daring. It's about you as a stylist not being afraid to take chances with combining colors, prints, textures, shapes, ideas and references. Ideally, successful styling tells a story and transmits emotions. When you style a client, think about the story you are telling, how you are telling it and how it is being read by the viewer. Pick up any issue of *Vogue* and you will see stories being told over and over again, year in and year out. The same thing can be done with clients. You just have to know the story to start with.

Your clients have specific clothing needs and, assuming you have been working with them for some time, you know their taste level enough to shop around for her. Stylists often have arrangements with local high-end boutiques to pull merchandise for their clients to try on. I frequently travel out of my way to find fun and hot fashion for my clients. I always take my own pull sheet (see Chapter 9 for a copy) to fill in when I take the clothes out of the stores. If what I take is one of a kind and expensive I will photograph it before I borrow it. This way the condition is recorded. I always have the manager double check my pull sheets to verify quality and quantity.

After I have pulled all the items for either the photo shoot or for the client, I merchandise them with accessories, shoes and jewelry. Be sure to have the correct sizes on hand (clothes, shoes, hats, jeans etc.) for the client (or the model). On occasion I have pulled merchandise and taken it directly to the client's house for her to try on.

If you are celebrity styling you will be approached by designers offering clothes to outfit your client for publicity purposes. Make sure you have agreements in place regarding fit, alterations, adjustments or any other changes you will need to make to have the garment fit and suit your client.

Of course, everything that isn't purchased by the client has to be returned to the store. Take the original pull sheet back and once again compare quantity and quality with the store manager.

STYLIST KIT

During the fitting with the client I will have my stylist's tool kit handy. This is a bag that contains the tools I need to adjust the clothes on the clients or the model. I include the following in my kit:

- Cell phone (duh!!)
- Pull Sheet – to fill-in and give to merchant/ fashion designer/ jeweler etc.
- Double sided sticky tape – to tape hems, hold fabric together strategically.
- Pins – myriad uses.

- Measuring tape – in case I need to measure another jacket from the rack while she is wearing one.
- Scissors – to trim away errant threads.
- Clamps or clothing pegs – to pull clothing tighter to show tailoring options.
- Gum and water – in case the client (or I) has a hunger pang.
- Kleenex – to shield lipstick from clothing during try-ons.
- Polaroid or digital camera to capture looks, quality of borrowed clothes.
- Pair of slip on nylon footie's – comfort in trying on shoes.
- Hand mirror – in case I don't have access to a three-way mirror client can see her back view this way.

STYLIST TIP

When styling think about your client and the 5 "F's":

FIT – make sure things fit as they should. Tailor them if they don't.

FUNCTION – is it appropriate for the occasion, event or job?

FIGURE – is the style congruent with her form (body shape)?

FASHION – does it suit her style personality and is it fashionable?

FRUMPY – does it make her look…fill in the blank…frumpy, old, outdated, silly, too young, too busy?

SAMPLE PULL SHEET AND CONTRACT

The following is an example of a contract for stylists. Some designers, PR agencies and photographers might supply their own. Be prepared to sign off on policies such as these:

1. All pull requests must be approved prior to scheduling.

2. All pulls must be accompanied by a letter of responsibility which must be either emailed or presented in person.

3. If a letter of responsibility is not available, a valid credit card number must be left on file for each pull. Please note that the credit card on file will be charged for missing samples within 5 business days.

4. All returns will be checked in while the stylist remains on the premises. Missing items will be documented, and copies of the documentation will be given to the stylist. Client is to be notified of every item that was shot and images must be provided as well as an issue date of the publication pulled for. If assistants are sent to return pulls, they must be apprised of this information.

5. All loans must be completely returned prior to pulling additional samples. If pieces from a previous pull are requested for an upcoming project, they must first be checked in, and then a new pull sheet will be issued with the pieces re-written.

6. Certain charges may apply for specific projects. Please note that this will be handled on a case-by-case basis.

Test shoots must be approved. Film and TV projects contracted first. Using the same merchandise for project and catalog shoots for clients other than those contracted is forbidden. In addition to the policies above, take digital images of each pull if items were worn or used. Supply information pertinent to press and PR associates.

PULL SHEET FOR PHOTO SHOOT

GILLIAN ARMOUR IMAGE
CORPORATE STYLIST

VENDOR/ CONTACT & PHONE	ITEM DESCRIPTION	SIZE	PRICE	CONDITION	RETURNED DATE/ SIGN OFF

NOTES:

PHOTOS ATTACHED_____SIGN, DATE, EMAIL

Notes:

THE THREE STEP CONSULTATION

The following guidelines take you through the simple steps of an image makeover. My method is based on the transformative steps I take my clients through. I have edited this guide down to 3 simple steps you need to take to complete a thorough consultation. Obviously you can add or subtract services as you see fit. Typically I set up three days of appointments – one day for each step of the consultation.

Meet and measure

In the initial stages of the consult, and even before you meet your clients you want to get relevant information from them such as contact numbers, emails addresses etc. Once you have met in person you can begin the intake and measurements. I recommend photographing the client to create a file about her and to record all measurements either on paper or in a database in your computer.

Curate (or shop)

In this section we explore the methods of closet editing, wardrobe styling and personal shopping.

Style and polish

Once you have completed steps one and two you can offer to help style the client with her new purchases, or with her existing wardrobe items.

Meet + Measure

CLIENT INTERVIEW

The initial interview is a great time for you to befriend the client. Of course, you should always keep your relationship professional, but as an image consultant you will need to know intimate details about your client (her weight, measurements, likes, frustrations, shopping habits and personal taste to name just a few). Your people skills will come in handy during this initial stage of the relationship.

Review:
    a) Client Application
    b) Client Needs Analysis
    c) Non-verbal Communication Review

SAMPLE CLIENT APPLICATION

NAME:
ADDRESS:
CITY / STATE/ ZIP
CELL PHONE:_____ **HOME PHONE:**_____
EMAIL ADDRESS_____

What is your profession?
How did you hear about _____ Image Consulting?
Why are you here today?   Fee discussed?
Please write a few words about how you are presenting yourself to the outside world through your appearance. *Add commentary to this description based on what you think others would say about your look. (Example: I wear a lot of black and I think that makes me look severe.)*

CLIENT NEEDS ANALYSIS – sample questions
    a) Why do you think you need image-related services?
    b) Have you ever had a makeover before?
    c) Are you in need of our services for a specific event? Explain.
    d) Do you have special physical needs that make it hard for you to wear certain things? (e.g.: I have fallen arches so I can't wear heels.)
    e) Do you want supporting consultations for etiquette, voice, mannerism awareness or visual poise?
    f) What do you think an Image Consultant can do for you?
    g) What do you hope to have learned at the end of your personal consultation?

Discuss: other questions you would want to ask your client.

NON-VERBAL COMMUNICATION STYLE

The following non-verbal communication points provide you an opportunity to effect change in your client and steer her toward success in life. Rate the client and make comments about your observations based on the subtle (and not so subtle) messages she is sending regarding her image and appearance. Be objective but not critical when you review these points with the client.

BODY LANGUAGE

- Stance (i.e.: confident, shy, etc.):
- Posture (excellent, needs work, poor, etc.):
- Greeting style (reserved, emotional, friendly, etc.):
- Eye contact (shape of eyes, low/medium/high contact):
- Handshake (loose, too soft, firm, too firm):
- Voice (tone, quality, and pitch):
- Language (accent, inflection, ability for small talk):
- Eye movement when in conversation:
- Body language (reflexive/non-reflexive/natural or forced)?
- Poise:
- Manners:
- Fashion style (defined, distinct, individual, confident, etc.):
- Communication component of dress (frazzled, clean, messy, etc.):
- Messages of appearance (economic, social, cultural):
- Energy level (mellow, depressed, hyper, etc.):
- Choice of color in clothing:
- Mannerisms or ticks:
- Body odor:
- Emotional expressions:
- Facial expressions:
- Quality of accessories:
- Labels or brands represented:
- Grooming:
- Makeup:
- Body modifications (tattoos, piercings, etc.):
- Smile quality:
- Self-esteem:
- Body confidence:

Other observations:
Did you notice areas that need adjustment or change? If so, then work with your client helping her make the appropriate changes to her image immediately. After all, the messages she is sending have an impact on how others treat her.

PHOTOGRAPH

Take before and after digital shots. Always take a headshot and a full body shot of before and after and keep as a record of the work you have done with the client.

Find a white wall in your studio. Using a digital camera take a close up shot of the client's face. Be sure her hair is pulled off the face (for accurate analysis later of her facial shape) and that she isn't wearing any makeup. Take a full body shot, without hands in pockets.

Hint: if you want a true "before" picture don't coach her first. Photograph her candid, as she is. See example above. Usually photos like this make for dramatic before and after results. Once you have the candid shot then:

- Have client take of eyeglasses.
- Have client relax and stand against white wall.
- Stand 8 feet away from her and sit on the floor to take a photo from a low angle.
- Take several photos, both front and side shots.
- Stand up for the close up of her neck and face. Take several shots. If she wears glasses take a shot with her wearing them and then a shot with glasses off.
- Remember you will be editing the background of these photos later so definitely stick with a white background for your photo.

When the client leaves and before your next session with her, edit the photos and file.

MEASURE TO DETERMINE BODY PROPORTION ANALYSIS

Date:_____ Client:_____

HORIZONTAL PLANE* BODY MEASUREMENTS:

1_____BUST — place measuring tape around chest at fullest part of bust line.

2_____WAIST — measure at the smallest part of the client's waist (do not worry about where the navel is).

3_____HIPS — measure the largest part of the derriere all the way around the body.

> Follow instructions on next page for vertical plane

4_____TOP OF HEAD TO FLOOR

5_____HIPS TO FLOOR

*A plane is used to describe the bodies position when standing. Horizontal plane describes lines of the body that are parallel to the ground. A vertical plane describes lines of the body that run from foot to head and are used to describe if a body is balanced or not.

STEPS FOR MEASURING VERTICAL PLANE BODY SHAPE:

1) Tack printer paper on wall 7' up (you will make your marks on this paper, not on the wall!).

2) Have client take off shoes and stand facing you (back to the wall).

3) Take the ruler and rest on their head so it touches the wall.

4) Mark a pencil (or pen) mark on the paper where the ruler meets the wall (should be at the top of their head).

This is their height_____

5) Now mark where their hips meet the wall.

This is their hip to floor measurement_____

This will determine their body balance - if they have a short torso, long waist, short legs or long legs and will help determine how to correct/ or camouflage any figure issues.

ANALYZE HORIZONTAL PLANE BODY SHAPE
Once you have your client's measurements you can use our online app to determine her body shape. While the point is to enhance the shape the client has, the final goal is to achieve the illusion of an hourglass body shape, which is considered the fashion ideal.

ANALYZE VERTICAL PLANE BODY SHAPE
If the client's hip to floor measurement equals exactly half of her height then she is balanced vertically. If her hip to floor measurement is less than half her height divided in half then her legs are shorter and hence her torso longer. If her hip to floor measurement is more than half her height divided in half then she has long legs and a short torso.

Examples:
Client is 60" tall
Her hip to floor measures 30"
She is perfectly proportioned

Client is 60" tall
Her hip to floor measures 26" (less than the 30" of height divided in half)
She has a longer torso
And shorter legs

Client is 60" tall
Her hip to floor measures 32" (more than the 30" of height divided in half)
She has longer legs
And a short torso

A balanced body shape is not the most common of the vertical shapes. However, it is the easiest body shape to clothe because there is no need to camouflage or trick the viewer into seeing a balance. With short waist and long waist shapes the goal becomes to create a balanced body shape. Use clothing silhouettes and lines to either raise the waist (for long waist) or lower the waist (short waist).

DETERMINING VERTICAL PLANE BODY SHAPE

Horizontal body shape differs from vertical in that it is a determination of the body circumference. Vertical body shape (hourglass, round, rectangle, inverted triangle, triangle) is measured across the planes of the body and is the space relationship between shoulder to bust, bust to waist, waist to hips. Measuring a client for vertical body shape determines whether she is short waist, long waist, short legged, long legged or balanced.

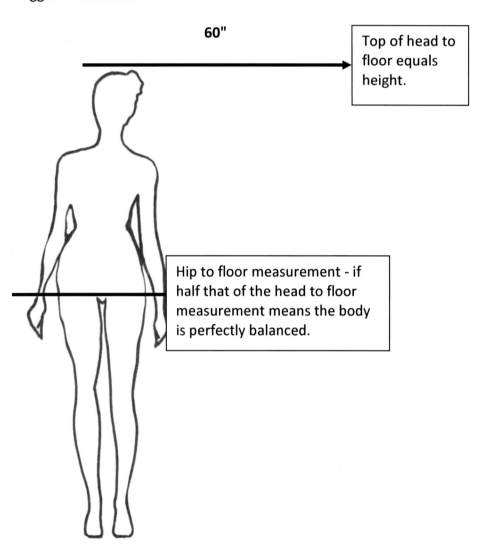

A more in-depth study of the vertical balance is included in our courses.

HOURGLASS BODY SHAPE

- Waist that is 9" to 13" smaller than the bust and hip measurements
- Medium to large bust
- Waistline is narrower than bust line
- Hips area as wide as bust line
- Horizontal figure type versus vertical type   (balanced)
- Has waist definition
- Has a proportioned body
- Legs are in proportion, but this body type may also have shorter legs
- Facial shape also rounded – either oval, long oval or round

An hourglass figure is the ideal body shape. If client has this shape she can wear many silhouettes and does not need to rely on clothing camouflage tricks to create a flattering figure. Choose clothes to wear close to the body. Baggy and shapeless styles do nothing to flatter this look.

If her body is proportioned, then she can wear lower cut waistlines on pants and has more room to play with clothing proportions. If not proportioned i.e.: torso is long or legs short, she will need to watch where to create the waistline in the clothes she wears. Hourglass shapes by nature are curved and curved body shapes will have curved lines that extend over the body. The facial shape will also be curved. One typically sees oval, long oval, and round shaped faces with hourglass bodies.

ROUND BODY SHAPE

- Rounded shape, fullness at midriff
- Smaller shoulders and full neck
- Shape created by weight gain
- No waist definition
- Bust, waist and hips very close in measurements
- Horizontal body line
- Legs are in great shape
- May have short legs combined with broad shoulders
- Facial shape also curved and rounded

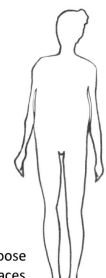

Proportion the top half of the body by wearing shoulder pads. Choose "V" necklines and vertical design lines (draped scarves, long necklaces, etc.). Floral prints work well as long as they are medium in scale, not tiny and not oversized).

Create waist definition with visual accents such as seams, darts and lines. Dark solid colors on the inside, lighter colors on the outside (like a two-piece suit with blouse underneath) work best as alternate outfits. Wear skirts only if they fall past the knee and with the same color hose and shoes. Wear bold accessories above the bust-line (pins, chokers, etc.). Avoid wide waistbands, cropped pants and oversized dresses (especially caftans or mu'u'mu'us).

TRIANGLE BODY SHAPE
- Small to medium size frame
- Narrow or sloping shoulders
- Hips wider than shoulders and bust line
- Body larger below the waist than above
- May have small bust line
- Large hips/ derriere
- Full legs, sometimes short legged
- Facial shapes usually with angles (square, triangle, diamond)

Balance the upper body by creating visual width - use shoulder pads and lighter colors on top, darker on the bottom. Wear tops with pleats, epaulets, ruffles, patch pockets. Wear simple and straight or slightly tapered pants without pleats or gathers at the waist. Draw the eye upward with colorful accessories worn around the neckline and shoulder area. Avoid adding visual emphasis to the hip area with long jackets. Choose jackets that are cropped or box style.

INVERTED TRIANGLE BODY SHAPE
- Shoulders wider than the hips
- Body larger above the waist than below
- Small hips and flat derriere
- Great legs
- May have full bust
- Clothes hanger shoulders
- May have short legs combined with broad shoulders
- Sporty/ athletic physique
- Facial shapes usually with angles (square, triangle, diamond)

Wear darker colors on top, lighter colors on the bottom. "V" necks elongate the upper body. If wearing loose clothing that falls from the shoulders, belt at the waist to define a waistline. Gathered skirts and flared hems look great on this body type. Wear wide legged trousers to create visual balance below the waist. Use horizontal stripes and patterns. This shape can wear halter tops well. Use accessories and jewelry to visually elongate the torso (scarves, long necklaces, etc.). Define the waist with belts or wrapped sashes.

RECTANGLE BODY SHAPE

- Hips and shoulders look balanced
- Very little or no waist definition
- Vertical body type (versus horizontal shape of an hourglass)
- Small or flat derriere
- Legs are usually long
- Waist measures 1" to 8" smaller than bust
- Very common figure type as women age or gain weight
- This body type also known as "square"
- Facial shapes have sharp and square lines (square, triangle, diamond, heart)

Camouflage goal is to create an hourglass shape; a small waistline. One sure way to do this is to increase the shoulder width at the same time adding width to the hips. This will create the illusion of a small waist.

Wear fitted jackets with defined shoulders (pads, lines, seams, etc.). Wear wrap dresses with waist accents to help create the illusion of a waistline. Wear gathers and pleats at the waist. Pants should be fitted with a slight flair at the bottom. Jackets with waist defining lines are good. Vertical lines will help elongate the figure. Depending on facial shape, wide necklines are also good.

REVIEW FASHION RULES WITH THE CLIENT

The following fashion rules for shape shifting are universal for all figure types:

- Black *minimizes* any figure shape.
- White *maximizes* figure shape.
- Small prints emphasize large shapes.
- Large prints emphasize small shapes.
- One color head to toe creates length.
- One color on top and contrast on bottom cuts a shape in half; it appears shorter.
- Too tight or too loose is always too wrong.
- Age inappropriate dressing emphasizes your age.

This is a good time in the consultation to review the *Clothing Guide for Body Shapes* (sold separately) with the client. It's also a great time to discuss her personal style confusions, problems, and challenges. Since she now knows her body shape it should be easy for you to illustrate (through photos, magazine clippings, etc.) appropriate styles and silhouettes.

Of course you will need to know how to camouflage any figure flaws your client has by using shape shifting silhouettes of clothing. We have discussed a few of them here (the five body shapes above) to give you an idea of how to do this.

The general rule when image consulting on body shape is to create the *illusion* of an hourglass shape for women regardless of their existing body shape. If your client happens to be an hourglass then the work is easier for you! Remember, the hourglass shape is the fashion ideal and has been for thousands of years. It is the only shape of all the female figure shapes that has the most pleasing visual harmony for the viewers eye.

What style points were used to visually shape her? What is her bodyshape before camouflaging? Discuss here.

FACIAL SHAPE

By looking at your client, in person or photograph, determine facial shape using the criteria below. Later in this guide you will choose hairstyles for her facial shape. Use these guidelines when determining client facial shape. Knowing facial shape allows the client to choose (and you to recommend) appropriate eye glass styles, hairstyles, jewelry and makeup tips.

OVAL FACIAL SHAPE - This facial shape is egg shaped. It can also be a long oval; think of a long oval as an elongated egg shape. This face shape is equal in size across the face horizontally and down the face vertically and as such is perfectly proportioned. If you have this type of facial shape you can wear many styles, shapes and sizes of earrings, necklaces, scarves and hats.

HEART SHAPE is wider at the temples and tapers to a smaller almost pointy chin. Across the face from ear to ear is one width and from hairline to chin length is longer. Faces in this shape can be proportionally balanced by wearing jewelry styles that elogate the face. Earrings can be long drops in angular shapes for maximum flatter!

DIAMOND FACIAL SHAPE - Women with this facial shape have wide jawlines that stretch out to their ears. Typically they have wonderful cheekbones. To proportion this facial shape with jewelry seek to balance out the width by increasing visual length. Long drop shaped earrings will flatter a diamond shape, as will long necklaces and scarves tied below the collar bone.

SQUARE FACIAL SHAPE - Face shape is angular and equally as wide at the forehead, jawline and cheekbones. To proportion the face with jewelry choose earring styles that draw attention vertically across the cheeks and continuing down the neck. Large chandelier shaped earrings work well for this purpose.

ROUND FACIAL SHAPE - This particular shape is wide throughout the jaw and cheek area, almost a filled out oval shape and can wear many styles of earring and necklace as long as the proportion of visual interest is vertical (to elongate the face) and not horizontal (which will widen the face).

TRIANGLE FACIAL SHAPE - has a wider jawline and narrower temple. The best jewels are ones that, when worn, will widen the face at the cheekbone. Earrings that are dramatic, bold, and big, worn close to the ear, are the most flattering for this facial shape. The best neckwear can include long necklaces to elongate the neck. Chokers and wrapped scarves do not flatter this facial shape.

Practice: draw facial shapes and add flattering hairstyles.

Curate + Shop

YOUR CLIENTS EXISTING WARDROBE

Your client's budget tells her that she cannot afford another thing, and besides her closet is already full of great clothes to wear. So what if some are last year's styles? The phrase that defines the new shopping trend -"shop your closet" - is apropos for the economic climate we're in. Most of us are saving our pennies and not investing in new clothes. Our old shopping habits have died, hard. Now it's time to "make do with what you have." Your client can still wear her old clothes this year – all it takes is a little innovation and creativity to learn how to style these old looks into new ones! Teach her how to re-fashion her existing wardrobe by looking at her clothing collection with newer, fresher eyes.

First, study current trends to get ideas
One of the best resources for studying clothing trends is online at style.com. Here you get visuals, trend reports and exciting video. Use these guides to determine the trends you want to appropriate for your client. Deciding which current looks she may like helps you work with what she already owns.

Next, "shop" her closet
Remember when you used to shop by season? Spring would follow winter and that was the time to purchase lighter sweaters and pastel colors. Then summer would follow spring and you'd go buy a selection of shorts, dresses and hot weather tops, not to mention sandals and hats and sunglasses! So let's follow this concept and pay a visit to her closet.

Think about the season you are in right now. As I write, it's summer and 90 degrees outside. My goal for dressing on days like this is comfort and coolness. Heading to my closet, I'm looking for breezy tunics and oversized shirts to pair with leggings. I'll also be on the lookout for shirtdresses, or long t-shirts I can belt and slouch over shorts or Capri's.

But by themselves, these pieces can be run of the mill. I want to switch up my styling and get a newer, fresher look out of these "older" pieces. Check out current magazines or online fashion sites to see what's happening in fashion NOW. When you see looks that appeal to you try to translate the looks for your client by using what already exists in her closet. For instance, last year's peasant blouses can be transformed this year by tucking them INTO jeans or skirts. Here are a few more last year/this year suggestions for your client:

- Last year's ombréd looks: layer them this year. Put a silk cami over last year's ombré tank top, then pair with mid knee leggings for a whole new look.
- Last year's oversize men's white shirt: add a colorful belt and an enormous/bold necklace. Wear over a pair of skinny jeans (also from last year).
- Last year's transparency trend – this year wear something over it.

You get the idea – develop your styling skills by reviewing last year's clothes and re-interpreting them into this season's hot looks.

Finally, much of fashion changes only slightly from one year to the next. Silhouettes are re-interpreted by designers to look fresh. Stylists take last year's looks and re-fashion them by tailoring or changing the cut of a jacket, pants or top to make them more relevant to today's trends. Your client can easily do this for herself with just a little guidance from you.

All she has to do is find a good alterationist or tailor who can help her achieve her vision. Have an idea in mind for converting the item you have pulled from her closet. Show her how jackets can easily convert to sleeveless vest styles. Skirts can be made longer or shorter depending on the mood of the fashion moment. Pants can be made into Capri's or shorts and even short-shorts if she is young enough to carry off the trend.

So, don't let your client's limited imagination stop her from getting creative with her closet – trust me, the minute you start helping her to look at her clothes in a new light her imagination will ignite and she will be able to create hot new looks. You'll be able to show her that she has tons of new things to wear!

THE CLOSET EDIT

Wardrobe editing is an important skill for you as an Elite Personal Shopper to master. Read on and put the following steps to work when you do a closet makeover for a client.

Step 1. Open the door
Step 2. Evaluate
Step 3. Decide
Step 4. Action
Step 5. Organize
Step 6. Celebrate & Close the door

Are you ready? Let's start. But first, set the timer, you are only going to be at this for two hours at the most. The best way to edit, purge and organize is to give yourself a time limit. Let your client know that this process will take patience. Sometimes I have clients do the first four steps on their own. Then I visit them to help organize, edit and determine what needs to be purchased to round out their outfits.

Step 1. OPEN THE DOOR
Take a deep breath and open the closet door. Here is where you will start the transformation of your client's closet. Take stock of what she has in there that really does not belong: e.g. the toy truck, the dirty towels, the laundry and even the dry-cleaning pile. These all have to be removed to be dealt with later in another way. Get as much clutter out of the closet as you can. Empty boxes, unused wire hangers? – toss them.

Now take a break and breathe. This next part is all about psyching yourself up to deal with what's ahead. If your client has attachment issues to her possessions, now is the time to tell her that it's all going to be OK. Nothing that she owns is so important that she can't let go of it.

So, now that you have opened the door, taken a deep breath and helped your client come to terms with letting go of some of the things that no longer serve her, it's time for Step 2, keeping the following *TEST* in mind for each outfit. Let it go if the client:

1. Has not worn it in over a year.
2. It never did fit (and it never will - how many of us buy things that don't fit us now but will when we lose those 5, 10, 15 pounds?)
3. It has never felt comfortable on her - every time she wears it she feels a little funny; she can't quite put her finger on it but she knows something isn't quite right.
4. She bought it on a whim and it is now completely out of style.

Step 2. EVALUATE
Review the clothes hanging in her closet with her. Take one item at a time and evaluate its worth, its history, and encourage her to begin asking herself these **5 QUESTIONS**:

1. Do I wear this?
2. Do I like it?
3. Does it still fit?
4. Is it in great condition?
5. Is it still in fashion?

Have her try things on to see if she still likes how they fit, feel and look. The goal of Step 2 will be to empty her closet into 4 piles on the bed or in the middle of the room, sorting each item as:

- FIX and/or ALTER /TAILOR
- DONATE
- NOT SURE

*The 4th 'pile' is **KEEP**; these items, and only these items, can stay in her closet.*

Step 3. DECIDE
Well done! Now that she has begun reconciling letting things go from her life, begin the process of actually deciding what to do with all that stuff. I want you to make three piles in the middle of the room/on the bed. One pile you will call "FIX", the next "DONATE" and the third "NOT SURE". The ones you have decided on keeping can remain safely in her closet (the "KEEP" pile: if A) they pass the **TEST** stated at the end of Step 1 and B) the **QUESTIONS** at the beginning of Step 2 are answered in the affirmative about each item). Now, one by one, take her clothes from the closet. While holding up or trying on each item, apply the **TEST** and ask her the **5 EVALUATION QUESTIONS**.

FIX Pile - If there are buttons that need to be sewn back on, zippers to be fixed, holes that need patching then it goes in this pile. If you find that it's really one of her favorite items but she hasn't worn it in a while because it doesn't fit, then it too qualifies for the FIX pile. You (or the client) will be taking all these clothes to a local tailor to have them mended and/or altered.

DONATE, or Give Away, Pile - This is the cemetery where all those clothes end up that don't pass the Step 1 **TEST** - she hasn't worn it in over a year, it no longer fits her, it always makes her uncomfortable etc. There are memories attached to these clothes, no doubt, so let her mourn them as you send them to the clothing graveyard. Once the clothes are in that pile do NOT let her pick them up, glance at them again, look them over to reconsider etc. Consider them a part of her history, gone, finito. They no longer serve her higher purpose.

NOT SURE Pile – The only clothes that land up in this pile are the ones that will force your client into Step 4, ACTION. Any item that doesn't belong in the KEEP, FIX or DONATE piles will go here. When she looks at that Christmas sweater from five years ago, remembering that it came from her favorite aunt; she doesn't really wear it anymore, yet hasn't the heart to throw it out – this is the pile for it. Or, it's the scarf she knitted as a class project in the fifth grade and it holds sentimental memories – yep, it too may go into the NOT SURE pile. Try to be brutal, try not to get hung up, but if your client really cannot let go right now, that's OK too (for the moment anyway).

Step 4. ACTION
This step takes her up the ladder of successfully reigning over her closet. It's time to take ACTION. Remember that FIX pile for mending and alterations? Take it to the nearest alteration expert and have them deal with it. If she is not willing to pay for the fix, then the item is not worth keeping. How about the DONATION pile of giveaways? Pack it up and haul it either to your nearest consignment shop (if she wants to make a few bucks on it) or donate it to a non-profit. And that last pile of clothes earmarked Not Sure? Well, she may not want to hear this but "when in doubt, leave it out". These clothes can also be donated to her favorite charity. Even though they have memories attached to them, they really are just clothes and no longer serve her higher purpose which is all about looking and feeling her best.

Step 5. GET ORGANIZED
So now her closet contains only the KEEPers! Doesn't it look better already? What's next? Well, you can suggest she upgrade her closet with a new structural design. If she has the budget for it, this can mean calling in professionals to help her. I had a client once who had her closet completely gutted, expanded and re-done so that she could walk in and find everything she needed. Her mistake was she waited until after construction was completed to call me in to help her edit her wardrobe. What a dusty mess it was! Before you call in the contractors, complete Steps 1 – 4 first.

You have already helped your client take the steps to purge, fix/alter or donate, and you have taken action where necessary. Now, what do you do with everything she is going to be keeping? Calling in a professional closet organizer is one possibility, or you can do it yourself. Either way, when done the client will now know where everything is and her closet will be organized the way she wants it. For instance, stacking boxes of shoes on shelves with Polaroid's attached is only necessary if she has a closet with 200 pairs of shoes. Most clients don't have anywhere near that amount, so simply keeping shoes where they can be visually scanned works just fine.

The simplest and fastest way to organize clothing uses a method called silhouette/ color sorting. The silhouette categories are pants, jackets, skirts, blouses, dresses, etc.

Put all like silhouettes together and then hang each category by color. Whatever color spectrum you use is up to you. When I do a closet edit I hang from white on one end to black on the other and the rainbow of colors in between. So, all reds are together next to all pinks and on and on. Now when the client gets dressed in the mornings she goes, for example, first to the pants rack, pulls a color, then moves on to the jacket rack, chooses a matching or similar color and finally it's over to her blouse rod where she pulls a contrasting color to round out a coordinated outfit.

Accessories should also be grouped by category as well. All purses on one shelf, all scarves hung on a rod, and so on. Because shoes can take up a lot of room suggest she buy a twenty pair canvas shoe holder (the kind that Velcro's over the closet rod).

Step 6. CELEBRATE AND CLOSE THE DOOR
Well, your client has made it this far, and, she has learned a lot about herself in the process. After all this hard work it's time to celebrate her victory – she is now the Queen of Her Closet!! Now, close the closet door, breathe deeply and congratulate her for a job well done. All in all this process should have taken you two hours at the most.

POWERFUL REASON TO LET GO
Go to any mall, supermarket, beach or Cineplex and you'll see it all - fanny packs, platform shoes, huge shoulder pads, dangerously long fingernails encrusted with plastic jewels. "People hang onto these trends way beyond their shelf life because they looked good in them once and think they still do", says Clinton Kelly, fashion expert and formerly the co-host of The Learning Channel's What Not To Wear. He says people stay with old trends because they have invested their money into them and don't want to spend any more. "Folks need to dig into their closets and let that bad stuff go."

ESSENTIAL PIECES

While the task of getting your clients closet into "best-dressed shape" may seem daunting, this list will help you find the essential pieces from her closet to help her build her wardrobe. List the essential pieces here, then use the 42 Piece Coordinates Form in the back of this book to complete a shopping plan. *Note that your clients core colors are the colors found in the irises of her eyes.*

Two dark suits in one of her core neutral colors

One dark skirt in one of her core neutral colors

Two pairs of slacks (or skirts) in one of her core neutral colors

Two solid shirts or blouses (not prints) in her accent colors

Two accent-colored shells that would look great under her suit jackets

A jacket that is tailored, yet loose, in an accent color

A knit shell in one of her core neutral colors

Complete this phase of your consultation with a review of what you have accomplished with your client up to now. Review the next pages of information with her to give her a better understanding of the process you are leading her through.

Investment Dressing
How often have you thought you had found a great deal on a blouse or a dress and bought it on a whim, only to get home and discover that it practically disintegrated with the first washing? All too often, we are taken in by these so-called deals that are really just low prices for low quality clothing. It is a waste of money and time as well. Spending $200 a month on these poorly constructed clothes means you are wasting $2,400 a year!

Investment dressing requires your client to pay more money per item of clothing, but she is going to be getting high quality items that will look and feel great and last a long time. The trick is to spot these smart buys that will help your client build up an investment wardrobe that she can use for years to come.

Know Her Colors
Help your client get her colors done. One of the smartest investments she can make to always look great and to not waste money when she shops is to get her colors professionally done so she can feel confident a color will look good on her before she makes a purchase.

Look for Timeless Pieces

There is something to be said for the little black dress that is appropriate for all occasions. If you look for clothing for your client that has lines that aren't trendy, but always look good, no matter the latest style, you have a winner. This includes pencil skirts, sheath dresses and simple blouses. These are items of clothing that could hold their own in any decade, not for being at the height of fashion, but for their simplicity and quiet class.

Go for Quality Fabrics

Paying more for clothing that is made of better fabric is a smart decision. In fact, the type of fabric used in the clothes one wears can make all the difference in how good one looks. A cheap polyester dress will look far worse than the exact same design in a classy linen blend. Choose the better fabric for your client's wardrobes and you won't regret it. Real silk, linen and wool are all fabrics that look terrific and will help her build her investment wardrobe. Blends are fine too. Wool blends will be less itchy, linen blends will wrinkle less and silk blends will usually breathe more.

Remember That More is Not Better

Having a few expensive, classic pieces of clothing in your client's wardrobe is worth far more than having two or three closets full of cheap clothing that will never pass as good quality. If you have traveled to Europe, you have probably noticed how great the men and women look. They do not have as many clothes in their wardrobe yet most everything they have is made of the highest quality.

Make It All Work Together

The best way to build your clients investment wardrobe is to plan her entire wardrobe for versatility. Having two or three pairs of pants, three to five blouses, a couple of skirts and a nice jacket and suit can actually work for her if you plan it. Choose just two or three classic colors that all complement each other and she'll be able to mix and match her entire wardrobe, creating dozens of different outfits. Throw in a scarf or two and a couple of different belts and accessories and she can have even more looks, all with just a few select items. Opting for mostly solid colors rather than prints will give your client more combinations as well.

Remember the Shoes

Choosing the best shoes available will also enhance her look. Invest in a few pairs of good quality, sensible shoes and she will be able to wear them with every outfit. A couple of different high heels, a pair of flat shoes and perhaps some boots or sandals, depending on where she lives, will serve her well and, when chosen in classic colors that suit her wardrobe, she'll never have any problems putting together a great outfit.

Investment dressing is becoming a trend these days and it's one that is well worth jumping on. Take a few minutes to plan out your client's basic wardrobe and choose a couple of colors to base it on. Then it's time to go shopping. Stick to the plan, choose high quality items; at the end of the day, she'll have a wardrobe that will last her a long time and suit any occasion.

Before you make that appointment to shop with her there are some things you need to know about going shopping and you will need to establish the spending level your client is ready for. This will determine where you and she will be shopping.

The following questionnaire makes it possible for you to have an open discussion with her about her shopping expectations before you make the shopping trip. Ultimately you will be the one choosing the stores to shop (you have established relationships or will soon) and you know the staff to work with. As you discover where she likes to shop you can choose to explore her favorite stores or, knowing her needs, you can direct her to places more appropriate to filling her needs.

What to look for when choosing where to shop:

- Ease of access: Is it too far away? Will traffic add to the travel time and cut into your shopping time together?
- Convenient hours?
- Convenient parking?
- Safe area?
- Good selection?
- Good fitting rooms and lighting?
- Helpful and friendly staff?
- Liberal return policy?
- Amenities such as free alterations, café, valet?
- Does the store keep you apprised about events, sales and new arrivals?

CLIENT SHOPPING FAVORITES

Favorite boutique? (local shops in local shopping areas)
Why?

Department Store? (Macys, Bloomingdales, Kohl's, Dillard's, Nordstrom)
Why?

Specialty store? (Saks, Bonwit Teller, Barneys, Neiman Marcus are examples)
Why?

Designer store? (typically stocks ready to wear collections DKNY, Alexander McQueen, BCBGMax Azria etc.).
Why?

Luxury store? (luxury stores are stocked with accessories and sometimes carry clothing (Gucci, Louis Vuitton, Hermés, Prada etc.).
Why?

Mass merchant/ Discount Retailer? (K-mart, Wal-Mart, JC Penney, Sears)
Why?

Shoe store?
Why?

I shop for fashion basics (jeans, t-shirts, sweats) at:

I shop for workout wear at:

Etc.:

ABC'S OF RETAIL SHOPPING

The Shopping Plan for the Personal Shopper

The next step in the personal shopping experience for your client is to make the shopping trip. You have already worked through her closet, developed outfits for her to wear, edited the clothes to be donated or repaired and made a buying plan to purchase items that will fill in the gaps in her existing wardrobe.

The key to successful shopping is knowing the environment you are shopping in. After many years in the retail world, I am well versed in the layouts of boutiques and department stores and have a few tips to share with you.

Boutiques

Small independent shops welcome personal shoppers through their doors. They realize the importance of the business you are bringing in to them. Plus, they are good strategic alliances for you to have. I foster my relationships with independent stores because I know they will give me courteous and friendly attention. Once you establish your relationship with them they are also great about keeping you informed of special events such as sales, trunk shows and new arrivals. These are all of interest to your client, but you should be the one that communicates these events to your client, not the store.

Be sure to protect your client relationship by explaining to the manager of the business that you are happy to bring clients in to shop their stores, but they are not to poach those clients from you. Most boutique owners will comply with you on this sensitive topic but it's up to you to make this point clear with staff from the beginning of your relationship with them.

Do not arrange to meet your client at the store before you. You should be the first to arrive to ensure that sales staff not encroach on your client by offering her shopping advice without you present.

Some of your clients will be rich and famous and love to get loads of attention when they shop. It's therefore important for you to work with the boutique staff by asking them to help you help the client. You can ask them to fetch clothes for you, to order in lunch, to get a bottle of water for your client etc. Any service you think your client might appreciate you can ask the staff to tackle. They, after all, will be getting the big sale and they are not paying you to make this transaction happen. Your client is paying you and while we are on this topic make sure the client knows ahead of time that you do not take a commission from the store.

Working with small boutiques offers another advantage as well. They are usually very willing to accommodate you for events you plan that involve them. I have done successful fashion show/ fundraiser events with small independents by inviting my client base to the store for the show and shop. Clients love this, the store loves it and it builds your reputation as an Elite Personal Shopper.

Luxury Boutiques
Keep in mind that this level of shopping only happens with high profile clients. You would not do a "shopping plan" in this situation. Shopping in luxury stores is something your client does for fun and if she has invited you along then you are there to shop with her, offer commentary, keep her focused on her sizes, silhouettes and colors.

Luxury boutiques will also welcome you enthusiastically. These brands (Chanel, St. John, Gucci, Prada to name a few) have built their success on great customer relations. They are more than eager to help you and your client find the best on offer. A few tips - do not be intimidated by this environment. Remember you are there as your client's **Elite Personal Shopper** and you are the person in charge of communicating your client's needs to the store personnel.

Staff in these luxury institutions are trained to work with very wealthy clients and as such will try to qualify the wealth levels by asking questions of your client. Gently let them know that you are the client's personal shopper and will be the only one in this shop allowed to work one on one with her UNTIL you give your permission for them to help. You then become the one who asks the questions of the salesperson. Your client will be looking and commenting and may alight on something that is of particular interest to her so then it is your job to ask the clerk to find the item in her size.

Department Stores
If you like a one-stop-shop these retailers are for you. If, for example, I have a client in need of a wide selection of items (and this typically happens on your very first shopping trip for her) such as lingerie, winter coats, boots and makeup then I will hit a large retailer. I can get all my client's needs met in one trip and that saves her time and money.

There are several advantages and disadvantages to working in department stores with clients. The advantages are that you have an enormous selection of items to choose from which makes shopping easy and that you are likely to be left alone by staff. The disadvantages are that you have an enormous selection and you are likely to be left alone by staff! The way to work around this is to have that shopping plan so that you are focused on what you need to find for the client AND to know that you might have to search for help when you need it. Department stores typically keep their staffing levels lean so don't be surprised if you have to hunt for someone to assist you.

Department stores are typically organized by size groups. You will find Plus Size (for curvier women), Petite (shorter women), Junior (for a younger body type), Misses (for a more mature body shape), Children's and Men's. This makes it easy for the consumer to find what they are looking for. Within each of these departments there are classifications of merchandise ranging from casual, sportswear, bridge, dressy, business, evening and designer.

Each of these "departments" have names and can be very confusing to the consumer. She may not know the difference between Bridge, Designer, Active Sportswear or Contemporary for example. It's your job to learn and know the definitions of these categories, the price points and the size ranges for each one.

This next chart is a broad overview of women's clothing categories. Be sure to visit stores often and take notes while there so you can better guide your clients when they shop.

Shopping report assignment here:

WOMENS CLOTHING CATEGORIES IN DEPARTMENT STORES

DEPARTMENT	CLASSIFICATIONS	SIZE RANGE	SPECIALTY
Designer	Casual Dressy Contemporary Sportswear Active Formal Intimate Evening Resort	00-14 36-46	- High end, higher price points - European styling, details and cut - Higher quality fabrics and details - Unusual styling features
Contemporary	Bridge Misses (Missy) Casual Dressy Sportswear Active Formal Intimate Evening Resort	00-16	- Moderate to better priced that feature forward looking styles - Fit to a more mature shape - Bridge is several price points above moderate - Missy is more state of mind and figure shape than age
Junior	Casual Dressy Sportswear Active Formal Evening Resort Outerwear	00-15	- Less expensive - Average age 14-25 - Younger, youthful styling - Fit to a less mature body shape
Petite	All options listed above	2-18	- 5'3" and under
Plus Size	Sportswear Designer Casual Dressy Active	0X-3X 12-24W	- Styling to flatter the larger woman - All age ranges - More expensive as this is a specialty product
Maternity	Sportswear Designer Casual Dressy Active	0-16 Use normal size add width to hips and waist	- Usually under age 35 so styling is youthful - Fit is comfortable - Sizes range larger in the waist and hips but carry the same sizes as contemporary
Denim	Found in all departments	0-16 XS-XXL	- 25" - 34" = waist - 28" - 36" = inseam

PRE-SHOPPING

Arrive at the store at least a half an hour ahead of her to pre-shop. (Yes, you charge for pre-shopping). Find the best and biggest fitting room you can. Introduce yourself to the department manager or sales person on the floor. Get the salesperson's name and work with him or her exclusively while you are in the department. Many clerks are on commission and will welcome the chance to help you find items for your client. Make sure that the area near the fitting room has a three-way mirror.

Visit the departments that are a match for your client (Misses, Juniors, Plus Sizes) and start to pull together outfits for her to try on. Remember to keep her seasonal color fan and her body shape analysis measurements in mind when you are pulling clothes.

You should also have the 42 Piece Coordinates Plan with you to keep you focused on what you are looking for. I usually pull five pairs of pants – jeans in dark denim, a neutral cotton, a neutral color wool, casual linen and a stretch khaki. At the same time, I choose blouses, tops and sweaters to coordinate with these pants. Then I look for three jackets that will match the five pants and the various tops. Make sure to check that there are extra sizes available in the item you pull just in case it doesn't fit when your client tries it on.

To save time while pre-shopping make sure to shop only the department that offers sizes your client fits into. Do not worry about accessorizing until after you have bought and paid for the items she will be keeping.

As you shop the department you may be approached by sales help. This is a good time to introduce yourself and to explain what you are doing. Ask to see a fitting room where you can set up all the items for your client. Also make it clear to the salesperson that when your client arrives on the scene you will be working with her and the salesperson is not to interrupt you at all.

Most sales associates get with the plan however, on occasion you will have salespeople that want to help out by offering their opinions and help. Gently make it clear to them that you are an Elite Personal Shopper and prefer to work alone with your client. Reassure the salesperson that they will get the sale and the commission when you are ready to have the purchases rung up.

Setting Up the Fitting Room - As said, try to find a large fitting room so that the client is comfortable. Take all the clothes you have pulled and then set up the fitting room with the clothes coordinated so she can try entire matched outfits together. Un-button jackets and un-zip pants so she can easily get into the clothes. Make sure there is a chair for her to sit on and that the lighting is flattering. If you think the setting isn't perfect your client will also. You want this to be a learning experience for her, not just a shopping experience. Once you have her trying on outfits encourage her to come out of the fitting room, so you can point out to her exactly what is and what's not working with each outfit she tries.

Shopping With the Client
Now you are ready to meet her. Starting in the lingerie department, get her fitted for an appropriate bra (9 out of 10 women wear the wrong size) that gives her the perfect body line for trying on the clothes you have picked out. While in the lingerie department, use the time and merchandise to teach her a few lessons about undergarment options. For instance, show her the section of Spanx® bras and shape shifters. She may not know how wonderful these products are for camouflaging figure issues.

Use all the time you have with her to teach and reinforce fashion rules. As you peruse the store, tell her about department store layouts: how departments are arranged by size; where this particular store has its restrooms, etc. Get her comfortable in this environment and make shopping an interesting and pleasant experience. Remember, for many women, shopping is a stressful and awkward experience. Not everyone loves shopping as much as you do.

*** Shopping Rule - do NOT shop for yourself on your client's time. If you see something you cannot live without, and this happens to me all the time, come back after you are finished with your client. Never let her see you shopping for yourself (or for any other client) while you are spending her time and money.*

When you arrive in your pre-shopped fitting room, let her know you have chosen several outfits for her based upon the information she gave you during your initial consultation, including her budget, needs and desires. Stand outside while she tries things on. Let her know that you want to see her in each outfit even if she thinks it looks terrible. Your time with her in the fitting room is an excellent opportunity to educate your client on the why's and why nots of clothing fit.

She will like some things you have chosen and reject others. Your job now is about going back and forth between her and the sales floor, finding other items that will mix and match. Never let her out on her own onto the floor. Time will be wasted, and she will be distracted. Keep control of this session by choosing clothing for her. Don't worry if she likes your choices or not. The whole idea is to get her into shapes that you feel flatter her and also to get her outside of her "safe" zone and into styles that she might never have considered.

As she tries each outfit, lead her to the three-way mirror. There, the light is usually better, and she gets a chance to see exactly how a garment should (or should not) fit. Describe how this line works for her body shape or how this particular color flatters her and, oh by the way, this jacket will go with many other things in her closet. Basically, you are selling her on these styles at the same time you are giving her your professional advice. Take the items she is finished with, both keepers and rejects, out to the salesclerk, who will process them for you.

This part of the shopping experience with your client should take no more than two hours. I find that any longer than this and fatigue sets in. I limit my clothing shopping trips with clients to a maximum of 3 hours. Offer to help your client shop for accessories on the next trip.

When she is finished trying clothes on and is ready to purchase, get the salesclerk's attention to complete the transaction. This is a good time to give the clerk your business card.

A Few Extra Tips
- Encourage your client to wear comfortable shoes, as you will be doing a considerable amount of walking and standing.
- Always start the shopping trip with a word to your client that you do not receive a discount or a commission for shopping a particular store and do not make any additional income from bringing clients in to shop.
- Give great customer service to your client and think of her needs the entire time you are with her. Carry her coat, her purchases and purse if necessary.
- Have a bottle of water and a snack, gum or mints with you in case your client gets hungry or thirsty.
- Have your stylist's bag with you: pins for pinning back items that need tailoring, masking tape for long hems, measuring tape and safety pins.
- Turn off your cell phone while with your client.

Above all, make the client's shopping experience with you an enjoyable and memorable one. She will use you again when she is ready to shop for the next season and will recommend you to others.

Always thank the salesclerk for her time and effort and get her card if you enjoyed working with her. Developing relationships with store personnel puts you into their loop and they will contact you when specials are available, so you can pass the information on to your clients.

AFTER SHOPPING FOLLOW UP AND DETAILS

Be sure to record all your clients purchases into the database you have set up for her in your computer. I keep careful records of clothes purchased, colors and sizes along with any information about shoes, jewels or makeup the client purchased. I usually do this while she is paying for the items, so I don't forget.

Follow up your shopping trip with a thank you card to the client. This is also a good opportunity to send her an interesting article or web link about upcoming sales events she may be interested in attending. Then keep in touch with her once a month via email and always send her interesting information. Do not bombard her with trivia that is of no relevance to her. Yes you are marketing for another shopping trip but do it professionally and tastefully.

Encourage your client to make shopping trips on her own using the tools you have given her (color fan, body shape books etc.) and mention that you are always available to edit her choices by meeting after she has pulled her own clothing.

Most of my clients contact me when they are ready to go for another shopping trip and I always do a phone interview before I set out to "hunt" for them. I always pre-shop before I meet the client. I have found that shopping with her and walking around each rack and each department with her commenting about what she likes and doesn't like is a time sucker. It's always best to have some idea of what she is in the mood to purchase so you can better plan what to pull for her.

As you develop your relationship with clients they will signal when they are ready for you to shop for them and without them. This is when it gets fun!! Discover their budget, clarify their needs and then set off to find what you think she will like. You must have prior arrangements with her regarding the financial aspects of purchasing. Will you be using her credit card account or your own? In which case you will need to keep careful track of receipts for purchases in case you have to return an item.

THE HOME STUDIO OPTION

Having your own studio is a great way to accommodate clients who are either too busy or too uncomfortable shopping in retail stores. Having a space of your own also gives you the opportunity to give a client a true fashion consulting experience. Since you will have shopped for her and stocked your studio with clothing items for her to choose from all that will be left for her to do is to try things on.

The best way to stock your studio for a client's personal fitting is to have an arrangement in place with the local retailer of your choice. You might have to enter into contracts with them so both of you are protected in the event that the clothes are damaged, stolen or lost. Some personal shoppers represent clothing lines such as Jana Kos, Carlisle and Worth and can invite their clients for seasonal showings.

When working with the retailer you need to arrange to borrow the clothes for your client to try on. I use a "pull sheet" when I am taking items from the stores I contract with. You can create your own custom form with your logo. Be sure to include all your contact information and have Kinko's create a triplicate form for you. One copy goes to the retailer, one to you and one goes back with the merchandise when you return it.

During the fitting make sure the items are fitting properly. Have pins and tape on hand in case you need to tweak a hem here, a cuff there. When the fitting is finished you will take these clothes to your tailor for altering.

A word about fittings in your studio: make sure you have a private space for the client to try things on. Don't use a bathroom! Have an area curtained off with a chair and a rack for her to hang things on. Keep the setting professional and comfortable for the client. She will also appreciate having a glass of water and some snacks nearby. Trying on clothes can get tiring!

YOUR CLIENT'S HOME

On occasion you will be asked to round up a selection of clothing for your client and to take them to her home for fitting. The same rules apply when you pull merchandise from the store for the client - use a pull sheet and have the items recorded by the manager of the store. If you are pulling expensive merchandise you can opt to photograph each item before it leaves the store. That way you have visual record of the items condition.

Bring a rolling rack with you when you visit your client and organize the clothes by silhouette (similar to the closet edit, pants together, jackets together etc.). Then show her how to coordinate outfits from the selection. Also have a full-length mirror available just in case she doesn't have one. You can buy lightweight portable full-length mirrors at places such as Target or Wal-Mart.

Have her try everything on and as she does so offer commentary regarding fit, function and fashion. This is another opportunity for you to educate her on the styles that flatter her figure shape.

When she chooses the items, she wants to keep write up a purchase order (or invoice), take her credit card information and head back to the store to return items the client did not want. Let the store handle the financial details and have them mail a copy of the invoice to your client. Keep a record of the purchase for yourself as well.

PERSONAL SHOPPING

What is an Elite Personal Shopper?
A Personal Shopper in a league of her own. She offers exemplary service to her clients, is creative and original with her offerings, is discrete, private and trustworthy. Shopping with her is always fun and exciting. An **Elite Personal Shopper** makes sure that clients book her regularly. She gets referrals from clients and associates all the time. Her target market is elite shoppers; women who are either self-made or in important social positions. Sometimes her client is aspirational, heading up the corporate or social ladder and utilizes Personal Shopper services for her family's needs as well.

Elite Personal Shopper as a career choice distinguishes you from whatever competition may exist in your neck of the woods. Branding and marketing yourself as an **Elite Personal Shopper** inspires confidence and trust. You have to back this title up with experience and this book aims to train you in the aspects of personal shopping that get you to Elite status quickly. This does not mean that you can forsake practicing on your own, in fact, I encourage you to get out and shop with friends and family before you start taking on paying clients. You will quickly learn how to apply my methods to suit your individual style and to tailor what you learn to fit the needs of your client.

What is personal shopping?

Some people love to shop for themselves and for others. Many have an innate talent for hunting and gathering the latest cool stuff. And then there are the professionals who make their livings helping others buy what they need. Personal Shoppers combine the natural talents of shopping, styling and consulting to help their clients look better, feel better and shop better.

Personal Shoppers are highly trained professionals whose job it is to shop for and with their clients. Shopping is a national pastime and for Personal Shoppers, it can be a full-time occupation. Professionals in this line of work have a keen fashion sense paired with an equally strong ability to recognize the desires and individuality of their clients.

Gaining experience as a Personal Shopper starts by working with friends and family. But how do you turn a hobby into a profession? Most Personal Shoppers start out in the fashion industry - working in various positions in retail sales, buying, advertising, and even journalism. I recommend you soak up all the knowledge and experience of the fashion industry you can. Doing so helps prepare you to launch your own dream career.

Successful Personal Shoppers KNOW how to shop. But they also know their first priority is their clients' needs and wants. Get to know your clients and develop relationships with them and they will always come back for your help.

How do you find clients?

Personal Shoppers need to be excellent networkers, publicity hounds and schmoozers (charmers) - growing your business means growing your client base. Great consultants create relationships, not just clients. A friend of mine in the financial world, a senior vice-president of a major financial institution, is extremely successful at what she does. Her secret? She doesn't have clients, not one. She has *friends*. Every one of her "clients" has a personal relationship with her. She cares deeply about them, their money, their family, their success.

And, to successfully target a market, you will need to define the demographics of your city. Go online and search for all the retail stores, fashion boutiques and hair salons within a five-mile radius of where you conduct your business. This is the list of businesses you are going to target when you announce your personal shopper service. These businesses become your strategic partners: their customers will become your new clients. See the Forms section for an example of a Strategic Alliance Worksheet.

Who is your ideal client and what does she do?
Ask yourself two questions. 1) Who is my ideal client? 2) What does she do for a living?

Just these two questions should focus you on who you want your client to be. Once you have her in your sights, you need to find out everything about her. What does she like to do for fun? Where does she live? What line of work is she in? What inspires her? Etc. Etc. The more you know about her, the more you can help her shop for all areas of her life. Get to know her style tastes and designer favorites. Because you will be shopping for and with her, you will also need to know her measurements, weight, seasonal color and body type.

What are some personal shopping myths?
It is a myth that Personal Shopping is something that anyone can do. *Shopping* is what anyone can do. But Personal Shopping is a professional designation. It takes training, practice and persistence to be a qualified Personal Shopper.

I have seen people who call themselves Personal Shoppers in action and I have felt sorry for the clients they are dragging around, almost hand holding the entire time. Walking around a department store while asking - Do you like this? What do you think of this item? Would you wear this? is a sure sign that an amateur is at work? These are questions a salesperson is trained to ask a customer. These are not questions you would ever ask your client. First because you have already established what she likes, doesn't like, what suits her, what fits her, and you know everything about her before she sees you at work and second, you would never waist her time and money by walking her around a store like this.

It's also a myth that Personal Shopping is a waste of time and money. The truth is the exact opposite; Personal Shoppers save their client's money and time by preparing and planning all purchases for the client. More money can be saved by shopping for investment clothing - something a professionally trained Personal Shopper is adept at. A master Personal Shopper, one with Elite status is so well versed on the layouts of stores that finding items to fit her client's needs takes minimal time and saves the client money as well.

MY GOLDEN RULES FOR PERSONAL SHOPPERS

1. Always be professional, discreet and do not gossip with your client or about your client.

2. Be enthusiastic, courteous, poised and polished.

3. Maintain the highest levels of customer service toward your client at all times.

4. Never over-dress for the client, your attire should be polished and professional.

5. Be knowledgeable about clothing, trends, designers, hot happenings.

6. Remember to treat all clients as luxury clients, give them the whole "elite shopper" treatment.

7. Never argue, the client is always right.

8. Remember that you are professionally trained and that your advice is based on your training. If your client doubts your taste and choices work with her to accommodate BOTH your opinions.

9. Your clients hire you; they are not personal friends. Maintain professionalism at all times.

10. Respect her time, her space, her finances and her goals.

11. Do not abuse the relationships you have with your key alliances (salons, stores, other professionals).

12. Communicate often with your clients and always have their interests in mind when you email, mail or telephone.

CAREER OPTIONS

Naturally there are many ways to structure your career as an Elite Personal Shopper. You could choose to be a solo-preneur (an entrepreneur working by him or herself), independent and freelance or you could opt to join a Personal Shopper service already in existence. Here are a few of the options available for trained professionals. I recommend that you get certified and join an association aligned with your career interests. The Association of Image Consultants or the Fashion Group International are two prestigious organizations that support the Personal Shopper profession.

Self Employed Personal Shoppers

If you are starting your business as a personal shopper, you will follow in the footsteps of entrepreneurs everywhere. They all started with a plan, a business plan to be specific. Having a business plan is the mark of a true professional. Research has shown that most businesses that fail in their first year did so because they lacked a clear, focused and attainable business plan. If you are going into business for yourself utilize the resources of the Small Business Administration in your city. Their services are free, and they are an invaluable resource for business owners.

When writing your business plan, you will need to detail as clearly as possible the following:

- Your business name
- The legal entity (sole proprietor, partnership, LLC, etc.)
- The business location - home office or shared office?
- What TYPE of Personal Shopper you want to be – Corporate Gift Shopper, Professional Executive Shopper or Elite Personal Shopper?
- Your target market - business executives, local celebrities, Mom's?
- Who your clients will be - educated, socialites, working professionals?
- Where will you find your clients? Advertising, referrals, friends?
- The amount of money you need to start your business.
- Where that money will be spent (advertising, materials such as stationery, business cards and brochures, etc.).
- How you will set up your office (computer, telephone, utilities – be sure to list your expenses in your business plan).

Be sure to read and fill out the Marketing Strategies spreadsheet in the Contracts & Forms section to familiarize yourself with the kinds of marketing activities you can use to promote your business. Being an entrepreneur can be hard work, so use all the strategies you can to get the word out about your business.

Employed Personal Shoppers
Working for a department or specialty store as an in-house Personal Shopper is a great way to break into this niche career. Most professional shoppers enter the business this way, get the experience they need and then go out on their own.

Department stores have Personal Shopper departments separate from the sales departments. Some have a team of shoppers. In-house shoppers are usually on salary, while some earn a commission on what they sell to their clients.

Shopping malls also employ Personal Shoppers. There are more options for shopping, and you represent all the merchants. Working for a mall will keep you busy.

Independent retailers hire on a contractual basis and are not as likely to hire full time personal shoppers.

If you are interested in being hired as a Personal Shopper, go online and search for companies that are hiring. Remember you will need some retail sales experience to qualify. Personal Shopper jobs are never entry level; most employers look for someone with a few years of retail sales experience and client relationships.

Online Personal Shopper – I created this service for my clients because in my neck of the woods, there are no high-end shops and the selection at local department and specialty stores is limited.

Working with clients in your office, at your computer, is both fun and time smart. A little planning makes the process smoother. Start with a one-on-one consultation for her needs and wants (just as you would do with any new client). Then you make a plan for what you will both shop for. You will have already pre-shopped online sites to see which are running sales, which offer free shipping, etc.

You must have personal experience with online shopping to be of help to your clients. Be familiar with shopping carts, coupons, shipping terms and online forms.

Sit comfortably next to your client in front of a computer (I have two monitors that share the same hard drive so we each have a good view) and click into the site you have both decided to shop. Go first to their size charts to match their measurements with your clients.

Online Shopping

- Always determine prior to your consultation the amount of time you will spend online. Keep your eye on the time. If you go over, be sure to let your client know that you are doing so. Let her decide if she wants to continue to keep you on the clock.
- Track the time you spend with your client, because you will be billing her when finished.
- When choosing items online, remember to stay within her budget and look for items that are in her seasonal color and body shape.
- Let the client complete the order form and payment process (keep it secure for her).
- Remind her to phone you if her purchases do not fit or if there is a problem. Keep this information for future reference.
- Send her notes when you see sites that she might like to shop the next time you meet.

Shopping Trip Tour Guide

I once heard Linda Buchman of the Shopping Sherpa give a talk at an industry event about her Parisian Shopping Trips and I thought that was the coolest job in the world. As Linda explained it though it sounded like a lot of work. But this is her passion and really when you work so hard at something you love it's not really work, it's fun.

Should you decide to start Personal Shopping tours find out if there is anyone already doing it in your area. You don't want any competition and you don't want to have clients who will compare you to your competition. Find your own niche. The retail shopping world is a big one, so you might decide to stick with shopping only malls or taking clients to certain neighborhoods.

A friend of mine does shopping tours of Union square in San Francisco. She schedules the tours to meet each Friday at a certain time. She takes groups of clients through the hottest and coolest stores within a four block radius round the fashion district. It's a little bit of exercise and a different experience from the one-on-one we have been focusing on in this book. But, again, it's an option and another opportunity to display your savvy shopping knowledge.

SAMPLE PERSONAL SHOPPER SERVICES AND FEE STRUCTURE

SERVICE	DESCRIPTION	TIME	FEE
New wardrobe shopping trip	Edit existing wardrobe, make plan, shop stores	5 hours	$175 per hour
Alterations delivery and pick up	Retrieve clothing items, fittings	2 hours	$150
Closet Edit	Steps 1-6	2 hours	$500
Shoe edit	Edit and organize shoe inventory	2 hours	$500
Jewelry and accessories edit	Edit, categorize, send for repairs, cleaning	2 hours	$500
Group shopping tour	For 10 - shopping trip, explore specialty boutiques, fashion show and shop	3 hours	$75 per person

INVOICE STRUCTURE OR ONLINE BILLING?

These days it is as easy as one, two, three click and your clients can pay for your services. Having an easy payment option for clients is key to the convenience of our service methods. I advise students to investigate the various payment options available online – from PayPal, the most common, to Stripe (the fastest) or even to Square – whereby you can make your iPad into a credit card terminal easily. Quickbooks and Microsoft are just two examples of the many document processing software options you can use to customize invoices, statements and order forms. Be sure to add all your contact details to your forms.

SETTING YOUR FEES

Every Personal Shopper charges a different fee. Some will charge per project, some by the hour and others charge a commission fee. Decide your fee's based on your yearly expenses and divide that number by the hours you want to work per day. That should give you a good estimate of the money you need to earn to cover your business expenses.

<u>Percentage of Price (commission)</u>
$25 plus 15% of purchases up to $1000
20% on purchases of $1000 or more

<u>Hourly</u>
$450 an hour or 20% of the purchase price (whichever is more)
(most Personal Shoppers charge in the $25-$100/ hour range)

<u>Daily Rates</u>
Full day (up to 6 hours) $500
Half day (up to 3 hours) $250
Hourly $100

<u>Per Project</u>
Full day of shopping, pulling merchandise to try on at client's home, closet edit and first fittings = $2500

The more experience you have and the more clients you get, the higher your fees should go. Don't price yourself out of the market, however. Do get paid what you deserve, remembering that even when working with high end clients, you cannot price gouge. A good rule of thumb on fees: reasonable + fair = return customers. Getting paid for your time also means you need to document and invoice your hours. I usually submit an invoice via email when I am finished with my client. Many Personal Shoppers keep their clients credit cards on file (with their permission) to bill this way.

KNOW YOUR CLIENTS

The chart on the next page gives you an overview of who your potential clients are, what their shopping style is, what their shopping needs might be and what you would typically find in her closet. When you can pinpoint your client's lifestyle in this way, you'll be able to shop to fit her needs easily.

CLIENT	SHOPPING STYLE	SHOPPING NEEDS	IN HER CLOSET
Celebrity	<ul><li>Luxury stores</li><li>Small, local boutiques</li><li>High end salons</li><li>High end gift stores</li><li>Custom tailors</li></ul>	<ul><li>Has specific needs</li><li>Limited time</li><li>Confidential</li><li>Private</li><li>Fast</li><li>Designer shoes</li></ul>	Designer One of a kind Custom Tailored
Socialite	<ul><li>Specialty retailers</li><li>Small designer boutiques</li><li>Trunk Shows</li><li>Fundraising events</li><li>Auctions</li></ul>	<ul><li>Occasion oriented</li><li>Special events</li><li>Gifts for family</li><li>Gifts for social events</li></ul>	Designer labels Exquisite vintage Heirloom pieces
Luxury	<ul><li>Neiman Marcus inner circle client</li><li>Private shopping events</li><li>Attends luxury store events</li><li>Group shopping with friends</li></ul>	<ul><li>Loves to take time shopping, loves quality items, not averse to a good bargain on occasion</li><li>Good jewelry</li><li>Designer shoes</li></ul>	St John Chanel Labels that are popular and recognizable
Executive	<ul><li>Contemporary and bridge department</li><li>Utilizes Personal Shoppers by phone and email</li></ul>	<ul><li>Is a planner</li><li>Does not like to waste time</li><li>Travel wardrobe needs</li></ul>	Armani Donna Karan Calvin Klein
Wife of Executive	<ul><li>Contemporary departments and sales racks</li><li>Online/Internet</li><li>Gift stores</li><li>Discount retailers</li></ul>	<ul><li>Frequently traveling</li><li>Social occasion dressing</li><li>Family event dressing</li></ul>	Rachel Roy Michael Kors Eileen Fisher DKNY
Working woman	<ul><li>Department stores</li><li>Small boutiques</li></ul>	<ul><li>Investment dressing</li><li>Needs clothing that coordinates</li><li>Shops her closet</li><li>Vintage and discount stores</li><li>Wash and wear versus dry clean only</li><li>Practical shoes and accessories</li></ul>	Skirt suits Selection of coordinated tops Comfortable pants Basic shoes Quality jewelry
The man	<ul><li>Specialty and department store</li><li>Discount stores for basic needs</li></ul>	<ul><li>Interview or job needs</li><li>Basics shopper</li><li>Catalog and internet on occasion</li><li>Gift shopping for staff and spouse</li></ul>	Suits Shirts Ties Shoes Jeans Overcoat

NEEDS, BUDGETS & PLANS

Finding her real needs isn't always an easy task. Discuss why she has hired you as a Personal Shopper. Give yourself about an hour to sort through her needs. Perhaps she is in line for a promotion and needs to upgrade her image and wardrobe. Maybe she has lost a LOT of weight and nothing fits anymore. Or, as may be the case when the economy is bad, she just lost her job and needs you to find an affordable interview outfit.

Once you have worked out the "why" and "how" of her needs, you will get to the financial basics. It is very important as a Personal Shopper to establish a budget BEFORE you shop. Never assume the amount of money she has to work with. You aren't being realistic if you think that not doing a budget is OK with your clients. Creating a budget and sticking to it are the mark of a professional Personal Shopper. Use the Budget Plan in the appendix (see sample on next page) to get clear about your clients current spending habits as well as her future clothing budget goals.

Planning what to shop for is also essential, in several ways. It focuses your client while you shop, AND it saves time for both of you. Start by reviewing the sample wardrobe plan on the next few pages. Create a worksheet like this to discuss with the client. The example is a clothing list, and you can use a similar spreadsheet with any other category of shopping needs.

Ask her about the gaps in her wardrobe, then fill in the boxes on your spreadsheet. Your first column might be headed "has" your second "needs" and the third column "goes with" (so you can offer her options and extend the use of her wardrobe).

SAMPLE BUDGET PLAN:

After you have sorted through her needs and the reasons she has hired you begin a discussion about her clothing budget. Use the form on the next page to get specific with her about the amount of money she spends now and the amount of money she wants to spend.

*included in your course are original forms for you to customize

	$25-$50	$51-$100	$101-$200	$200-$300	Over $300
I spend $					
Per Jacket				☑	
Each Pant		☑			
Pair Jeans			☑		
A Skirt			☑		
A Blouse				☑	
A Dress				☑	
Evening Item					☑
Pair Shoes	☑				☑
One Bag					☑
Jewelry				☑	
I want to spend $ on:					
Per Jacket	☑				
Each Pant	☑				
Pair Jeans	☑				
A Skirt	☑				
A Blouse		☑			
A Dress		☑			
Evening Item			☑		
Pair Shoes			☑		
One Bag		☑			
Jewelry		☑			

SAMPLE WARDROBE PLAN:

Here is a simple 9-piece grid to use when planning a coordinated range of outfits. Nine pieces in just three colors will create 42 separate and coordinated outfits for your client. Use this grid when planning coordinates. You can Xerox this form, fill it out as you go through her closet, discover any holes (needs column) and then plan to shop (to buy box) for her.

ITEM	Blouse	Short Sleeve Top	Shirt/Jacket	Jacket	Pant	Skirt	Pant	Dress
Has	Red sleeveless	Black tank	Red jacket	White Jacket	Black pant		Denim Capri	Sleeveless denim
Needs	Black blouse	Red print		Red				
To Buy	Fitted black blouse	Red or black print top to match other pieces		Red Crop		White skirt maybe denim		One or more- perhaps white background print

Then take this list with you when you shop. I always have a list and a plan before I go shopping. Master shoppers know that this is the only way you can shop for and with a client. You never want to be on the selling floor while she is with you and you haven't got a clue as to what you are looking for. This makes you look unprepared, unprofessional and she will quickly assume you are wasting her money (and time).

COLOR MAKES AN IMPACT

If you haven't already done a color analysis for your client, you will need to do so before you begin the shopping trip with her. If you do not have certification in this specialty you can easily locate someone who does. Do an online search in your area for "color analysis" and see who comes up.

Alternately you can take your client to the cosmetic's department of your local department store and have her skin tone tested.

Your clients will be either cool or warm based in their skin coloring. Naturally the clothes you put them in will have to match this underlying skin tone. You can short cut color analysis training if you have a color wheel and study how to determine cool and warm colors. This method is not without risks as you will not have a trained eye to determine color by sight when you are shopping with your client. This could prove to be risky for your professionalism not to mention embarrassing if, for instance, you chose incorrect colors for her. I highly recommend that you get trained in color analysis before you begin working with clients.

Once you are certified in color analysis you can train your clients on the importance of color and the impact colors can make when worn correctly. Colors can leave psychological, emotional and mental impressions on the viewer, so an awareness of the impact color has on others is important for your client to study.

HOW AND WHY TO MEASURE THE CLIENT

Use the following charts to gather the information you need about your client. You will need a measuring tape or wall chart, (preferably both) and a scale.

Measure	List Here	How	Because
Height		Shoes off stand against wall, hold a book on top of clients head and mark where the book meets the wall	To determine proper proportion and fit of clothing
Weight		Use a scale or ask client	To determine proper proportion and fit of clothing
Bust		Wrap tape around chest at largest part of bust	To determine proper proportion and fit of clothing
Waist		Measure around the smallest part of waist	To determine proper proportion and fit of clothing
Hip		Take measurement around largest part of hip (buttock)	To determine proper proportion and fit of clothing
Arm		Actual measurement from 1" below armpit to wrist bone	Sleeve length on jackets etc.
Sleeve		Measure from top of shoulder to wrist bone	Length and fit of tops, jackets etc.
Front Neck to Waist		From base of neck to waist indentation	To determine fit of tops and jackets
Back Neck to Waist		From nape of neck to waist indentation	To determine fit of tops and jackets
Width of Back		Measure 4" below shoulders from armpit to armpit	To determine fit of tops and jackets
Waist to knees		From waist indentation to mid knee	Determine proper fit and length of skirts
Waist to ankles		From waist indentation to below ankle	Determine proper fit and length of pants/ shorts
Wrist		Measure circumference above the wrist bone	For best jewelry fit
Head		Measure around the forehead	For hats, accessories
Shoe		Measure from heel to top of big toe for length, widest part of foot for width	Best fit
Ring fingers		Use a ring guide	For best jewelry fit
Neck length		Base of ear to collar bone	For accessories and jewelry fit

SIZE CHARTS

Keep in mind that women's standardization of sizes has never been successful, so clothing sizes will vary depending on the maker or designer. You must always try clothes on your client and do a thorough fitting session with her. If she is not with you when shopping use your measuring tape to get accurate sizing. Don't go by the number on the label or tag.

PRACTICE MEASURING HERE

Measure	List Here
Height	
Weight	
Bust	
Waist	
Hip	
Arm	
Sleeve	
Front Neck to Waist	
Back Neck to Waist	
Width of Back	
Waist to knees	
Waist to ankles	
Wrist	
Head	
Shoe	
Ring fingers	
Neck length	

Style + Polish

CLIENT REVIEW SESSION

No matter how many flaws your client may have, or thinks she has, she also has assets. The best way to look great is to downplay her body flaws and accentuate her assets. For example, if she has great legs, but is a little heavy in the hips, opt for a slender skirt in a darker color to minimize her hips and still show off her nice legs. Likewise, if she has a good chest and a not so great stomach . . . use a plunging neckline to show off this asset and distract from that little bulge. Find ways to draw attention to her best parts and she'll find that she looks and feels better.

Use Color to Change Shape

Your client's body is probably not perfect – not many are. But a little color goes a long way toward creating the look you want. Dark colors slim, while light colors tend to expand, and bright colors draw attention. Use this to your advantage. If she has a triangle-shaped body, with wide hips and a narrow top, try using dark-colored pants with a light top to balance things out. A bright scarf will draw attention away from the wider hips. This color principle will help you choose clothing to create the perfect look for her.

Find Flattering Cuts

When choosing pants, look for a cut that will enhance and balance her body type. A small waist and hips look great with tapered pant legs, while a large bottom can be slimmed by choosing a flared skirt or boot cut pants. Likewise, a crisscross or ruffled top will enhance a small chest by adding more bulk, while a plain shirt with only darts will look great on a larger chest. Peasant shirts, which are more flowing, flatter a smaller torso and fitted tops look better on larger women.

Use Accessories to Your Advantage

Accessories can be your client's best friend. Not only do they help distract from areas you don't want people noticing, they can really add flair to her wardrobe and help to make her clothes look better on her. For example, if she is tall and wants to look a little shorter, a wide belt can help create that illusion by providing a "cutting" line at her waist, which stops the eye. When the eye can move the length of the body without interruption, this creates the illusion of length, and so it stands to reason that a belt that creates an interruption would cause the body to appear shorter.

Knowing how to choose clothes that enhance your client's body type will result in a boost in her confidence. She will end up wearing outfits that look excellent on her body and leave her feeling great. The best way to get started is to use the above guidelines to get rid of any clothing that doesn't suit her body type and then hit the stores to find something that does suit her. Once she has redesigned her wardrobe, there will be no more wondering which outfit will look right on her . . . everything will be just right.

ALL ABOUT FIT

These days sizes on tags mean little since the actual sizes vary so much between designers and different clothing lines. Recognize that it does not matter how gorgeous or well-made a garment is, if it does not fit your client properly it will not look good.

Unfortunately, most women do not know how important it is to get a good fit and as a result, they have a wardrobe full of pretty, yet unflattering clothing. The solution is quite simple: get clothes you buy to fit you properly. The following tips will provide you with the knowledge necessary to find clothes that fit and flatter your client's body, no matter what size she is. With the right clothing anyone can look stunning.

Find Out Her Real Measurements

Do not mentally rely on those measurements you took a few moments ago. Knowing a clients real size in inches is vital to getting a proper fit, so get out the tape measure and take those measurements again. Write them down so you'll remember and be sure to check your clients measurements at least every six months so you can shop for the right fit.

Look for Width Before Length

If you are going to have to alter your clients clothing, it's almost always easier to shorten than it is to change the width. So, when you are doing your shopping, make sure that the clothing you select fits around her properly even if it's too long. For example, jeans that are a perfect fit in the hips and waist are almost always too long for most women. This can be altered and, in fact, many stores offer this service.

The part that matters in her pants is the waist and hips, since these are the areas that people will be noticing and, of course, it is also important to feel comfortable. For shirts, the shoulders and chest are the important parts. Even if the sleeves are too long, or the waist is too wide, this can be altered as long as the shoulders are in the correct position and she has no pulling in the chest area. The sleeve seam should hit the edge of the shoulder, as opposed to hanging down the arm or being too close to the neck.

Use the Right Foundation Garment

When you go shopping for new clothes with your client, it's important for her to wear the proper undergarment to try on clothes. Don't recommend she use a tummy flattening panty if that is not what she would normally wear under her clothing. A good bra is essential, particularly if she is large-chested, since she will need to see precisely how tops hang when she is well supported.

Aim for Fitted, Not Skin-Tight

There is a saying – "skim, not skin" – that works well when you are choosing clothing for fit. Clothes should not be like a second skin; they should fit close enough to look good, but not reveal every bump and lump on your clients body. On the other hand, baggy clothing is most definitely not flattering either, so try to get something between too loose and too tight. Just skimming the body is ideal.

Find a Good Tailor

It is fine to drop off your clients pants at the dry cleaners if they need a hem, or if a shirt needs shortening at the sleeves. However for her jackets, suit pants, and outfits for dressier functions, find a good tailor. Ideally you want one with experience, someone who really knows how to modify a garment. Depending on her body shape, you may, for example, need to take the shoulders in on every jacket to get the best look; this is not an easy job so you want to have a tailor you are confident in to do this delicate work.

A LITTLE MORE ABOUT TAILORS AND SEAMSTRESSES

A seamstress/alterationist is someone who can tailor (verb) (fit it to your body) and alter clothing, fix any damages to clothes and sometimes create custom designs. A tailor (noun) is someone who custom designs, creates and fits clothing for both men and women. Sometimes they do fixes but it is not their forté. A dry cleaner cleans clothes and sometimes fixes the holes, missing buttons, falling hems, and so on.

When working with a seamstress, it's important to trust that they know how to pin and tuck to fit. Your job is to let them know during the pinning/fitting when you feel comfortable in your clothes. Their job is to adjust things to your liking and sew away. Expect to wait a few days to get your "new" clothes back. And remember to try on your items before you pay; if there are adjustments that were missed or that hem wound up way too short, you'll be able to leave that piece to be fixed again. Soon you'll have a bunch of "new" clothes that are ready to impress.

Excerpt from Merriam-Webster's Dictionary

THE TEN RULES FOR MIXING AND MATCHING PRINTS

The rules of art and design are also the rules of fashion design. Fashion styling, as an adjunct profession of fashion design, calls on stylists to employ these principles and elements to create successful images for clients.

What gets left out of the textbooks and other art training resources is the important fact that all great imagery tells a story. In this chapter I review the Ten Rules that are THE most important for you to know when you are high styling.

Image: FGI.org

After this section on the Ten Rules I will tell you about the importance of tone, mood and story - the final parts of putting the cherry on top of a great outfit combination.

When you begin mixing and matching patterns, prints, moods and shapes, don't be afraid to experiment. Getting the combination of principles and elements correct every time you style is a lofty but difficult goal so the more you practice, the closer you will get.

First buy a mannequin and use it to style pieces from your own closet. Then go shopping and choose a range of fun prints to work with. Take photographs of each outfit you style and begin to build a photo-folio. If you are paying attention to the design rules we have reviewed in this book, then chances are you will be mixing and matching successfully.

Invest in a color wheel to take with you when you are practicing mixing and matching. That way you stay in the color ranges that work. When using color remember to use the rules of color listed in the following pages of this book.

©Fashion Style and Image Consulting

1. Use the same color (and temperature) family of prints (ex: *muted cool* family grey/blue). A family of colors look "related" to each other and share the same hue, temperature or shade. For instance: a family of gray colors could consist of steel gray, blue gray, purple gray and olive gray.

Notice the four colors that make up the coordinated outfit (below and on the next page). Each of these colors has a dusky, muted look. When they were mixed there was a touch of black added to give them this smoky appearance. Each one of them is from the same family AND they are complementary (appearing opposite each other on the color wheel).

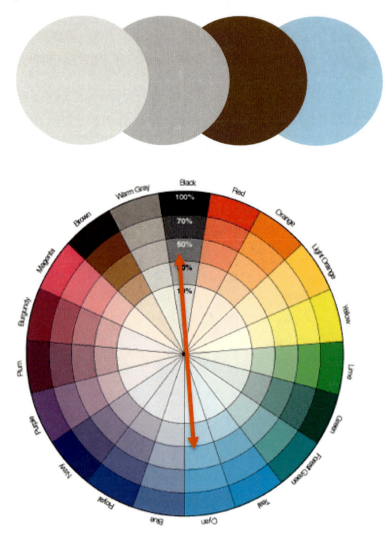

©Fashion Style and Image Consulting

Exercise: describe the color family (example: dusky, bright, earthy etc.) represented in this collage. Add your own collage with descriptors here:

Coordinated colors should come from the same TEMPERATURE of the color wheel. The color wheel is a system of colors arranged to follow the scheme of colors, a rainbow for instance, that occur in nature. This wheel is divided into cool and warm based colors. Half the color wheel has blue (cool) as its base undertone (also called temperature) and half the colors have yellow, a warm undertone. As you examine this color wheel notice the division of cool and warm colors along with the percentages of saturation that occur when white is added.

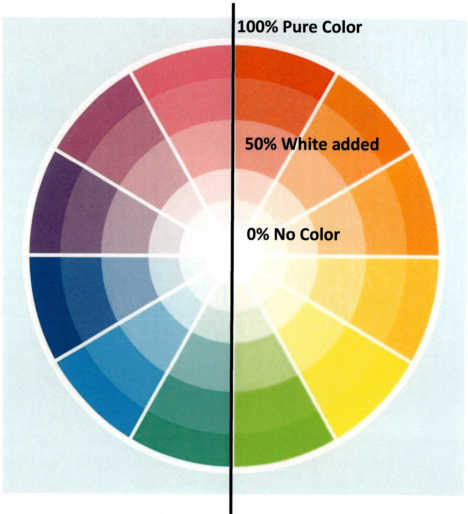

When prints and patterns are mixed to create a successful visual image they are almost always from the same temperature family on the color wheel. This rule gets broken, as we shall see later, when using square color combinations in interior design.

2. Pair a neutral (or solid) print with a busier print (red is considered a neutral, notice the drops of red in the print that match with the textured red neutral). Textured fabrics can act as "prints" if the texture is dominant, as in this example below:

3. Use combinations of scale, weight or balance (small, medium and large) of print with the same background color:

Small Scale   Medium Scale   Large Scale

4. Use prints to draw the eye away from, or to, a focal point.

As with color, prints with high contrast can draw attention where you want or don't want it. Printed fabrics with dark backgrounds will act to decrease the visual size of a shape, so, using a black background fabric with white polka dots can visually decrease a large bust on a woman. Conversely - using a fabric with white background and dark print overlay will increase body size. If a client has a large bust, you would NOT put a white blouse with black polka dots on her.

5. Repeat colors within an outfit (a white shirt, white and black tie paired with a white pinstriped black and gray jacket) and use just one chosen color to bind all the other coordinates together. As in the following examples, the solid shirt is the unifying color.

6. Use similar "lines" throughout the outfit - straight lines with straight, and curved with curved, so the lines are repeated in each fabric print:

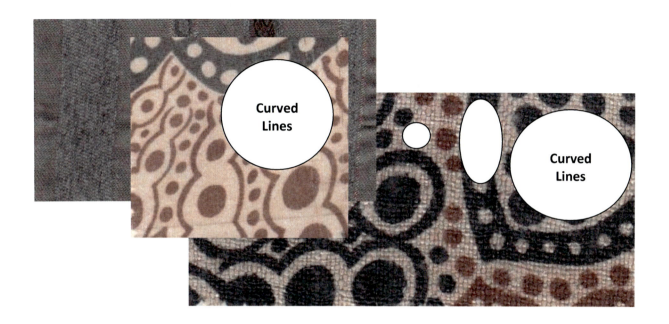

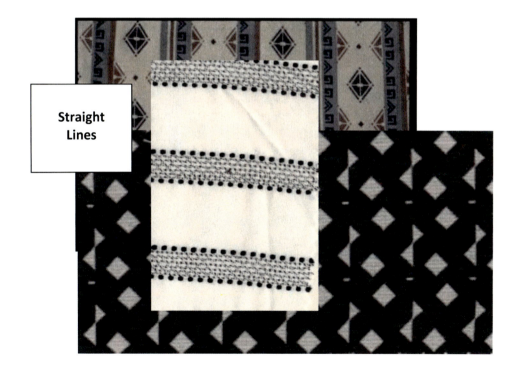

7. Mirror similar elements (shapes, sizes, details) from same color temperatures:

Ex: this pinstripe shirt pattern has a ¾" space between each stripe, likewise the anchor logo on the tie is ¾" wide, and, both the vertical stripe and the vertical direction of the anchor pattern mirror each other. Also note one more element: the mint green stripe sitting within the cool blue pinstripe is in the same *temperature* as the kelly green (cool) tie.

Cool Color Temperature with Stripe Pattern

Here you can see patterns in facial features mirrored in fabric patterns and hair style. This "harmony" of elements creates a balanced visual image as seen in the mirrored and repeated "pattern" of circles below (more about lines in facial patterns in #9):

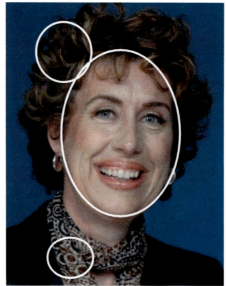

8. Wear a larger print where you want more attention and a smaller print where you want less attention.

Images: Fashion Group International

Exercise: define the elements or principles used in the creation of the outfits above:

9. Small, medium and large-scale print should *relate* to body and bone structure size. If a woman is large boned she can wear large scale prints, details and style lines. If small boned then delicate, small patterns, lines and details work best. Note: solid colors are considered "small" print.

Take a look at the face shapes on the next page and identify the dominant lines in the face. By analyzing dominant "lines" in facial shape you can make correct decisions about the best lines (curved, straight or both) to use in the clothing choices for the client.

	Identify Lines	Facial Shape	Scale of Features

Examples of Small Scale Prints	Medium Scale Prints	Large Scale Prints

10. Combine opposing lines and elements only if there is an element in common:

Example: combining circles and stripes works in this illustration because the element in common is the black background of all three fabrics.

So, there you have the Ten Rules for mixing and matching prints, patterns and styles successfully. I recommend you start practicing by collaging cut-outs from magazines, photographing interesting combinations you see in department store displays and watching what people are wearing on the street. And consider getting a mannequin and starting your own photo-folio.

In the next section I will review some the basic color rules for creating mixed and coordinated color stories. If you don't already own a color wheel you can get one at your local office or art supply store. I like the miniature ones from **www.colorwheelco.com** - they fit easily into my pocket and go shopping with me!

Color Combinations

There are only six basic ways to combine color into successful and compatible clothing coordinates. Use them to create harmonious combinations of color in the outfits you style.

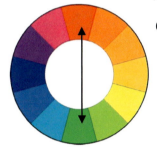

Complementary

Colors that are opposite each other on the color wheel are complementary colors (example: red and green). Because of the high degree of contrast use these colors to stand out or make a statement. When stylists refer to contrasting colors, they mean colors opposite each other on the color wheel.

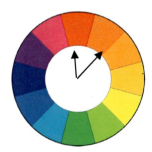

Analogous

Analogous color schemes use colors that are next to each other on the color wheel. They usually match well and create serene and comfortable designs. Analogous colors are often referred to in styling as "monochromatic." In styling these neighboring colors are considered low-contrast.

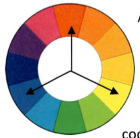

Triad

A triadic color scheme uses colors that are evenly spaced around the color wheel. Triadic color harmonies tend to be vibrant, even if you use pale or unsaturated versions of hues. When styling triadic harmony successfully, colors should be carefully balanced - let one color dominate and use the two others for accent. In fashion triadic color combining is used to create coordinated outfits.

©Fashion Style and Image Consulting

The use of triadic combining does break the rule of using the same temperature (undertone) of color to create outfits. Using cool and warm colors in triadic combining works only if two of the colors are in one family and the third color is used as an accent (or for friction).

Split-Complementary
The split-complementary color scheme is a variation of the complementary color scheme. In addition to the base color, it uses the two colors adjacent to its complement. Because this scheme creates strong visual contrast it's best worn on high-contrast skin-tones.

Rectangle (tetradic)
The rectangle or tetradic color scheme uses four colors arranged into two complementary pairs. This rich color scheme offers plenty of possibilities for variation in styling. Here is an example of a tetradic scheme:

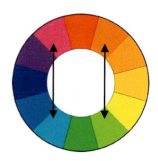

Square

The square color scheme is similar to the rectangle, but with all four colors spaced evenly around the color circle. Use four colors to create visually interesting and coordinated outfits. Square combining is often seen in menswear and interior design features.

The best way to learn how to mix and match colors using the coordination and combination rules above is to practice. You can also look at photos in magazines or at clothes hanging in a closet to contrast and compare the combinations that seem pleasing to your eye. Be sure to look for outfits that are compatible in one of six ways diagrammed above.

EXECUTION

Creating Successful Visual Images with Mood, Theme or Story

It's enough to know about the principles, elements and color rules when mixing to match. But it helps to pay attention to the other components of creating successful visual images in print combining - mood, theme and story.

As a fashion stylist and image consultant I keep my eye on the personality of my client and, even as I am reaching to shake her hand at our initial meeting, I am making a mental note of personality clues. I am trying to get a read on who she is as a person, so I can build a vision of how I want to style her; a vision based on her authentic personality.

Then, when I am ready to style her, I look for combinations of colors, prints, patterns and clothing styles that suit her personality. I accent the look with accessories that also speak to her authentic style.

I start this process by keeping a story in mind for the vision I have for her. You will find your own method of building a story through mixing and matching; just be sure to keep in mind all the principles we have been reviewing in this book.

For example: if my client has a sunny, bubbly personality and I know she likes vintage clothing, the beach and vintage crosses, I am apt to create a story that speaks about sunshine, cute styles and fun prints (see photo). The story for the vision would match her personality and could then be interpreted into an outfit.

When fashion designers start the process of creating designs for a new season they often turn to favored sources of inspiration to create a mood (theme or story) for their collections. So, too, should you when you are ready to mix and match successfully.

You can find inspiration by studying, for instance, art books, architecture, history, other fashion designers, museum shows, vintage stores. The basic goal is to find a story to tell through the clothing worn.

It's not always necessary to know the personality of a client to tell a story through clothing. When I work a photo shoot it's my job to put the clothes on the model and to choose accessories that speak to the concept (vision) the client requests. If the client wants me and the photographer to interpret her vision of, let's say, fox hunting, then I would style the clothes with a leafy background and add accessories to put a finishing point on the tale. I might also find a few riding crops and riding boots to finish out the vision and add a step and repeat fox logo in the background for fun.

The same pertains to fashion imagery - telling a story based on ideas and concepts makes an outfit come to life. If you study any one of the women (or men) who made the best dressed list this year you will see stories being told. Look at any editorial layout in Vogue magazine and you'll also see stories unfolding.

Take a look at this photo and describe a vision/story about it in the text box below (don't over think - write whatever comes to mind). Think of a setting, a situation, a story about these objects:

Based on the story you created about these objects try to visualize a three-piece mixed and matched outfit that defines the story through clothing and sketch it here:

Practice and Train Your Eye to Identify Successful Pattern Schemes
Understanding how to mix colors is essential to creating an effect that is both pleasing and harmonious. To get ideas, look for color schemes you find attractive in not only fashion spreads and ads in magazines, but in fine arts, paintings, and nature.

Take Cues From Interiors:

List all the colors you see in this photo:

Now describe the prints you see:

About.com offers a few simple tips to mixing and matching interior print combinations. The same principles and elements of design are used.

- Keep the background colors the same when coordinating patterns (for example all white or all ivory)
- Repeat colors in each pattern
- Include a mix of pattern sizes: large, medium, and small
- Add plain or textured fabrics for more interest

Taking Cues from Men's Wear
One of the most popular field trips we take in my Fashion Stylist class is to the men's department at Neiman Marcus, a personal favorite of mine because it is the only luxury department store in our area that features a broad selection of European menswear. It is from the European menswear designers that the experience of viewing mixing and matching in all its glory can be observed by students of style.

Taking a walk through we see "man"- nequins dressed in combinations of check, hounds tooth, stripe and square patterns all blending into a unified whole. This is the essence of high style and we can learn a lot from the abundance of creativity at play here. The Italian designers, Etro, Zegna and Versace all play with mixes of pattern and color.

We can learn lessons from the guys and apply them easily to women's wear outfit selection. Here are a few ideas:

1. Select a range of sizes for prints and a range of background colors geometric, bold, striped, dotted.
2. Work with multiple fabrications; houndstooth, pinstripe and intarsia.
3. Don't be shy about mixing up fabrics (textures) and prints (patterns).
4. More than four print and color combinations is too much.

Describe why and how these combined patterns work together:

Pull Outfits Together Based On Four Coordinates:

1) **Main** - the most dominant item of clothing - usually what's on top.
2) **Accent** - the color that ties together the basic clothing item with the neutral.
3) **Neutral** - typically the final item of clothing, usually a basic pant, skirt or short.
4) **Accessory** - the color of an item that ties the outfit together. Scarf, jewel, handbag, or shoe.

Additional key points to remember when coordinating clothing include fabric and style. Each of these elements make up a successful outfit and each one must be accurately coordinated. Here are the guidelines for successful coordinating:

Fabric - textiles play an important role in the clothing styles of today. Natural fabrics have made way for synthetics as the easier choice for wear and care. Careful use of the correct fabric can make a dull outfit exciting or an exciting outfit dull. Match personality of fabric to the construction of the garment; for example - an elegant evening gown made out of casual cotton would look strange. Better to use a formal fabric such as silk or velvet to match the formality of the garment construction.

Style - how an item of clothing looks. Typically explained by its personality - smart, sophisticated, casual, formal. Prints and patterns must match the personality (style) of a garment. Example: a cherry print would look awful on a tailored jacket. Pinstripe (formal pattern style) looks perfect on a tailored (formal style) jacket.

As with clothing - accessory coordination must be in harmony with the color family of the main outfit. If you are accessorizing a cool colored outfit stick with cool colored accessories; likewise warm colors.

Jewelry colors vary from the basic metals to the myriad versions of semi precious stones but, the same rule of harmony applies.

There is more leeway in styling when using accessories because you can play with artistic styles and creative textures. Accessories by definition add spark to an outfit and so should make a statement. Don't be afraid to play with ideas when accessorizing.

Fashion Styling - Creating Outfits That Work: Cluster Wardrobe Exercise

Now let's review how to build a wardrobe using clusters. This is one of the most effective strategies you can use to build a wardrobe that works. You can use it to guide your purchases generally and it is also very useful for meeting specialized needs.
For example, it is the perfect way to create a travel wardrobe, a business wardrobe, or a wardrobe for a specialized activity.

Clusters were originally used by department store buyers and fashion manufacturers to plan the selling floor pad each season for merchandising groups of new styles. They are used to this day by manufacturers as a guide for fashion buyers planning their buys. Wardrobe clustering was eventually introduced to the consuming public with great success in helping plan personal shopping trips.

A wardrobe cluster is a group of garments with a minimum of five pieces and a maximum of 24 carefully chosen to coordinate with each other to build a mix and match wardrobe of many pieces. When you build a wardrobe using 'clusters' of garments you can create maximum versatility and flexibility with a minimum number of individual pieces. So why would we want a wardrobe that was built around the cluster concept?

The benefits of using this technique to expand a wardrobe include:

- More outfits using fewer pieces
- Save time and money
- Achieve a put-together look
- Can add more pieces over time to expand even more

When you build a wardrobe using 'clusters' of garments you can create maximum versatility and flexibility with a minimum number of individual pieces.

To begin your cluster you will need at least 5 garments, but to make the cluster concept really work you will, over time, be adding garments to that initial foundation. If you have thoughtfully selected those original 5 pieces it will be easy to make additions to your cluster. You will have a clear sense of what additional purchases will best expand your options and it will be easy to keep an eye open for 'just the right' next purchase.

As you make those additional purchases, the cluster wardrobe guidelines will inform your decisions. Rather than buying just anything that catches your eye, you will be making purchases that expand the scope and range of your cluster. Each time you add a piece the number of wardrobe combinations you can create will expand geometrically.

Theoretically, a cluster could expand indefinitely, but usually somewhere between 15 and 24 individual garments will give you maximum versatility. At that point you can begin to think about creating another cluster, ideally one that will have some overlap with your existing cluster.

As outlined above, using this strategy offers a number of benefits:
- If you are able to 'mix and match' the individual garments in your wardrobe in a variety of ways you extend the scope of your wardrobe. You can have many more options, many more looks, with the same number of pieces. We all need a variety of clothes that can take us to a range of activities and venues.
- When you need fewer pieces to meet your wardrobe requirements you can get by with a smaller financial outlay. Working within a structure that helps you define what you are shopping for helps you save time when you are in the store. You can quickly focus on the few items that might possibly make a good addition to your cluster. Having fewer pieces to care for also saves you time and money when maintaining your wardrobe.
- Perhaps the greatest benefit to building your wardrobe around clusters is that you will always look put together. Taking the time to create a master plan and then making purchases consistent with that plan will ensure a polished appearance.
- Over time, your cluster can expand with a minimum of effort as you add a piece at a time. You're not starting from scratch each time you make a purchase. Instead you are purchasing a garment that will be used in a variety of ways with the existing pieces in your cluster.
- In our busy lives anything that can introduce a note of simplicity is a benefit. Deciding what to put on in the morning becomes a much simpler task when your wardrobe is organized around the clusters.

Begin With Five Pieces

To begin your cluster, you will need to select a minimum of five foundation garments. As we said before, we're not talking about just any five garments, but five garments that have been carefully selected to work together. It is vital that each foundation piece works with all the others. Over time as you begin to expand your cluster by incorporating additional garments you will have greater flexibility in your choices and you will be able to select garments that work with only most of your other pieces rather than with absolutely everything. But for these first five pieces, each individual garment must combine with each of the other four garments. This will provide a solid foundation for your cluster. The exception to this rule is that pants and skirts will obviously not be worn together.

Select a Palette - Pick One or Two Neutral Colors

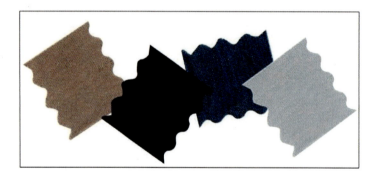

Your first decision will be to select a color palette around which to organize your cluster. Begin by selecting one or two neutrals. These colors will become the backbone that holds your cluster together. Some of the most basic and widely used neutral colors include Black, Light Grey, Charcoal, Navy Blue, Beige, Khaki, Brown, Olive Green, Taupe, Camel, Ivory, White. Other neutrals might include: Burgundy, Cinnamon, Mauve, Forest Green.

©Fashion Style and Image Consulting

Select a Palette - Pick an Accent Color

If neutrals provide the backbone of your cluster, it is the accent color you select that provides that little splash of energy that keeps everything interesting. Generally speaking, accent colors are lighter and brighter. They come closer to being pure hues. Many people are quite content to dress in predominantly neutral tones but introducing a small amount of an accent color will enliven your wardrobe.

Color is a strong communicator and the judicious use of an accent color will bring added interest and energy into our wardrobe. It also provides the means for making a more personal statement of style. Using colors that reinforce your personal coloring, your eye, skin or hair color, for example, has the effect of enhancing your visibility and presence.

Accent colors play a supporting role and include:

- Bright Pink
- Bright Green
- Yellow
- Orange
- Bright Blue
- Bright Turquoise

Select a Palette - Add a Print or Pattern

A great way to find and incorporate an accent color is with pattern. You can do this

by finding a pattern that coordinates with your neutral color choices yet also introduces a new accent color. A blouse or shirt in a patterned fabric is an obvious good choice. For men, ties provide an opportunity to use brighter, bolder colors and for women, scarves are a ready source of bolder color. Note that all the items we've mentioned succeed in introducing these brighter, bolder accent colors in small controlled amount near the face.

Medium to Dark Colors

Relying on medium to dark neutral colors has several advantages:
1. The medium and darker neutrals are appropriate any season of the year. Even in the warmer summer months the darker tones can be combined with brighter, lighter colors in your wardrobe to create a fresher more seasonal effect.
2. The medium and darker neutrals will require less frequent laundering or dry cleaning. This makes them easier and less expensive to care for.
3. If you happen to weigh a few pounds more than you would like, the darker hues have the added advantage of creating the illusion of a slimmer, trimmer figure.
4. The darker hues will also give the appearance of a higher quality garment. Slight irregularities in construction, wrinkles, or subtle evidence of wear will almost always be more apparent in a light fabric than a darker one. You can, of course, still introduce an accent color to enliven the outfit. The second-from-left model, wearing a coral and brown color palette, is a good example.

Rely on Separates

Another cardinal rule for building a wardrobe using a cluster strategy is to rely on separates. Separates will make it possible for you to create the maximum number of different looks from the minimum number of individual garments. If you had five dresses how many different looks you could get? You could get five and no more. But with five separates you will be able to combine the individual pieces in a variety of ways. This is the key to creating versatility and scope.

How Many Make a Cluster?

An ideal sample five-piece cluster could contain:

- Two tops
- Two bottoms
- One layering piece; vest, sweater, or jacket

KEEP IT BASIC AND SIMPLE

When choosing separates remember to keep it simple and keep it basic.
There are several elements that determine how a garments rates on the 'basic and simple' barometer test. They include:

- The silhouette of the garment
- The interior style lines
- The fabric (print or pattern)
- The detailing and embellishment

Of these two skirt options; the blue, tweed pencil skirt would make the best choice to be included in a basic five-piece cluster. Its silhouette is simpler. The fabric, while having a good deal of surface texture, is much less distinctive. The color, the pattern, and the full gathered silhouette of the skirt on the right would make it much more difficult to pair it with a variety of other garments. The white oxford shirt is another example of simple and basic. The fabric, the silhouette, the color and all the detailing are classic, plain and uncluttered. By contrast, the blue layered blouse, while very lovely, is far from basic or simple. The fabric is sheer and layered. There are soft ruffles at the neckline and sleeve hem and the body of the

©Fashion Style and Image Consulting

garment is composed of little decorative pleats. You can see how the blue blouse would be much more difficult to combine with a variety of other separates. While it is gorgeous, it would not make as versatile a choice to begin a cluster.

Even the most casual of wardrobes can be built using the cluster concept. Here are   two versions of the classic blue jean, but in the pieced version the simplicity of the design has been interrupted by the surface treatment. The patchwork design, with added seams and color, creates a very busy, patterned effect and it limits the ways in which we would be able to wear the jeans. While these are fun and make a very lighthearted casual statement, you would not be able to create a business casual look, for instance, with these jeans. The classic blue jeans, on the other hand, can more easily be dressed up. They would look equally good with T-shirt and with a cashmere sweater and suede blazer.

Everything Now Coordinates

Let's take another look at the five-piece cluster we began with. As we said before, we're not talking about just any five garments but five garments that have been carefully selected to work together. When you begin your cluster, it is vital that each piece works with all the other pieces. This example gives you a good idea of a balanced selection of pieces with which to begin building a wardrobe cluster. These five garments would provide a solid foundation to build around.

Notice that each garment will work with every other garment. (The skirt and the pant are the only exception.) What's more they can be combined in a variety of layered options. Let's see how many different looks we can create using just these five pieces.

Pants, Jacket, Shell and Shirt Combination

Let's take four of our five pieces, the pants, jacket, shell, and shirt, and look at the various ways we can put them together. We'll look at four groupings or sets of garment combinations, each with a different theme.

The theme for this first set of options is the pantsuit. These examples all use the pants and jacket to create a suited look. But notice how much variety we get using only these four basic pieces. We go from a tailored, conservative look to a more youthful, casual look and we do it using the same wardrobe pieces, but we have put them together in different ways. Remember that one of the goals in building your wardrobe around a cluster is to create maximum variety using the minimum number of pieces. In our example, the pants and jacket were purchased together as a suit, but they could have been purchased separately.

Pant, Shell and Shirt Only

Now let's look at some additional combinations. We are still using the pants, shell, and shirt but now we have eliminated the jacket. Though we no longer have a suited look, we still have wardrobe options that would be appropriate in many workplaces as well as for a more casual venue.

Four Pieces Make Seven Options!

Using only the pants, jacket, shell, and shirt we were able to create seven interesting outfits. This grouping represents approximately half of the possible wardrobe options available using our original five pieces. But even without introducing the skirt you can see how we have managed to create variety and scope.

©Fashion Style and Image Consulting

Skirt, Jacket, Shell and Shirt

Now we take off the pants, figuratively speaking, and see what happens when we add the skirt. These four options all create the look of an unmatched suit with skirt. It is a look that would be appropriate for business, church, community activities or leisure time.

Shirt, Shell and Skirt Only

By removing the jacket, we can create these three additional looks. Again, because we have eliminated the jacket, the look is less professional, but it would still be appropriate for many workplace situations.

And here are the seven great outfits we've put together using just four pieces; the skirt, the jacket, the shell, and the shirt!

©Fashion Style and Image Consulting

And here you have it all! Look at all the looks you get by combining just five pieces! We have put together a closet full of wardrobe not just a closet full of clothes and we've done it all using only five basic pieces. We have created outfits that would be appropriate for a job interview and outfits you could wear to the movies. Part of what makes this approach to wardrobe building so useful is that it helps you to easily create outfits that will take you everywhere you need to go in your daily life and it does it with a minimum investment of resources.

Accessorize

One of the ways you create variety with only a small number of pieces is by adding accessories. You can change the mood and feel of an outfit simply by altering the accessories you choose.

Add a Belt, Scarf or Jewels In this example, the model has added a belt. The look can go from fun, casual, and youthful to more traditional and conservative simply through altering a single accessory.

Expand the Cluster

Now that you have a good idea of how to go about selecting the foundation pieces for a cluster, you are going to get a chance to practice the principles you've been learning. Together we'll look at a series of garments and accessories and I will ask you to choose the best pieces to add to our original cluster. Consider the color palette, the color value, and the design elements of each of the pieces as you make your choices. As you make your selections remember you are building on our existing cluster, adding garments that work back to each or our original five pieces.

If you were making these additions you would likely be adding a piece at a time as your budget allowed and as you found the appropriate garments. Always remember to look for the highest quality garments you can afford; it becomes easier to afford quality when you limit the quantity. Always look for garments that are distinctly different from those you already have. If you have a grey skirt already, don't buy another grey skirt. If you love grey skirts this can be a real temptation but try hard to resist or you will be seriously limiting the versatility and variety your wardrobe cluster can deliver.

Add One Sweater

Consider both of the pictured sweaters in relationship to the original five-piece cluster. The Icelandic sweater would introduce a new sporty element to the cluster. That's a plus. The blue cardigan, however, unlike the Icelandic sweater, is a layering piece. It can be worn over the blue shell to create a twin set effect. It can be worn over the blue and white striped shirt, and it can be worn under the black jacket.

Patterned Sweater **Cardigan Sweater**

Adding the Icelandic sweater would create only **two** additional wardrobe options (sweater+skirt, sweater+pant). Adding the blue cardigan would create **six** additional options (sweater+shell+skirt; sweater+shell+ pant; sweater+shirt+skirt; sweater+shirt+pant; sweater+jacket+skirt; sweater+jacket+pant).

Add One Skirt

How about adding another skirt? Consider these two options in relationship to our existing cluster. Our options are a long floral print or short blue denim.

The floral skirt could be worn with the black jacket, but it would not work well with the striped shirt. While it could potentially be worn with the shell or the cardigan, because there is no blue in the skirt, it would not create a well-coordinated look. While the lack of color harmony would appeal to some, others would find it unworkable.

Chiffon Print Skirt **Blue Cotton Skirt**

Some might argue that the floral skirt would be a good choice because it brings a new soft feminine element to the cluster. This is a good argument but if the floral design incorporated the blue hues of the shell and cardigan it would make the floral skirt a much better option. So, the best choice here is the blue cotton skirt for a cluster addition.

©Fashion Style and Image Consulting

Add One Blouse

How about adding another blouse to our cluster? Let's say we've decided to purchase a white shirt. It will go with the pants and both skirts, the jacket, the tank, and the blue cardigan. And here are the two options we must consider. They're about the same price and quality, and they both fit well.

But which of these two blouses would you want to add to your cluster? In this exercise, unlike the previous two, there is no absolute right or wrong answer. Each of the blouses has pluses and minuses.

Option #1, the ruffled blouse, is a silk and rayon blend. It is a dressier fabric than the blue and white striped shirt we already have in the cluster. For that reason, it expands the scope of the cluster by introducing a more formal, elegant element. But the ruffles down the front and on the sleeves also add a more complex design element and though the blouse is classic it is not as basic in design as option #2.

Option #2, the tucked front blouse, is a more tailored cotton shirt. Its fabric and style are closer to our original shirt. That is both an advantage and a disadvantage. It is an advantage because its simple silhouette will combine easily with all our other pieces; it is a disadvantage in that it doesn't bring to the cluster an entirely new element as option #1 does. Blouse #2 can also be worn open as a layering piece and blouse #1 does not lend itself to being worn in that way.

Remember Those Accessories!

Now that we have expanded our original five-piece cluster by adding a sweater, a second skirt, and an additional blouse, it's time to think about accessories. We aren't ready to leave the house in the morning without, at minimum, shoes and some type of purse. We usually have shoes and purses in our closet already that will work with any new cluster we begin but let's assume that in this case we are truly starting from scratch.

Which of these three purses would you select to add to the cluster we have just created? Did you choose the perfect one? Or not:

Bag#1 – Too casual, trendy and fun to be a first choice. It would make a good second bag to add to the cluster. Color Palette does work.

Bag#2 – Color is too light in value to be the best first choice with the darker tones of the pant, jacket, and skirt. Using the accent color for accessories is a good idea but again, not if it is your only accessory.

Bag#3 – This would make the best choice because it is the darkest neutral color of the cluster palette. It is also a classic, simple design. The materials, leather and metal, and the quality construction also make it the best choice as a first purchase.

Cluster Wardrobe Re-Cap

When you begin to build a cluster and select your original five foundation garments, you want to have a balance between tops and bottoms. It obviously wouldn't work if you had five tops or five bottoms. It wouldn't work much better if you had four bottoms and one top.

A good balance for a foundation five-piece cluster would consist of:
- 2 tops
- 2 bottoms
- 1 vest, sweater, or jacket

A balanced cluster composed of eight garments might include:
- 3 tops
- 3 bottoms
- 1 jacket
- 1 sweater or vest

And finally, a workable twelve-piece cluster might consist of:
- 5 tops
- 3 bottoms
- 2 jackets
- 2 sweaters or vests

BODY SHAPE MEASUREMENT CHARTS

- **HOURGLASS SHAPE**
- **ROUND, OVAL OR DIAMOND SHAPE**
- **TRIANGLE BODY SHAPE**
- **INVERTED TRIANGLE BODY SHAPE**
- **RECTANGLE BODY SHAPE**

Please visit the online app stores (Apple and Android) to download your free version of our measurement charts. Available in both metric or standard measuring format, this easy to use phone app speeds the bodyshape determination session with clients.

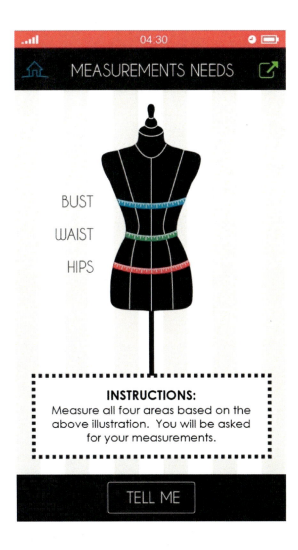

©Fashion Style and Image Consulting

GILLIAN ARMOUR, AICI CIP

Image Consultant /Celebrity Stylist and fashion columnist. Gillian appeared for several seasons on the Emmy award winning NBC show *"Dream Makeover Hawaii"* as its official image consultant and stylist. As a Style Director Gillian has produced fashion shows, photography shoots, TV commercials and TV Movies. She has styled many celebrities and teaches certified courses to budding Fashion Stylists and Image Consultants on campus in Sacramento, California. Gillian takes pride in being the pioneering creator of on-line Image, Style and Fashion e-learning courses. She continues to expand the image industry by certifying students globally.

Her career in fashion reaches back 25 years and includes executive, managerial and buying positions with retailers **Macy*s, I. Magnin** and **House of Fraser**, London and manufacturers Jessica McClintock, Esprit, Byer, Fritzi (My Michelle/ YouBabes) and her own brand GA Design. Gillian is the author of 18 books on image and writes for successful fashion social networking sites. Gillian was recently named a beauty expert for several high fashion magazines and blogs about fashion, style and image frequently.

Website: www.FashionStylistInstitute.com

Email: contact@fashionstylistinstitute.com

REGISTER and ENROLL

If you are not already registered in our courses and are viewing this manual at a friend's house perhaps then follow these steps to be certified as a fashion, image, or style professional today:

1) **Visit www.FashionStylistInstitute.com**
2) **Navigate to the courses menu.**
3) **Choose the certification training course you want to enroll in.**
4) **Read the details on the page (details, objectives, units and materials).**
5) **Click the payment button, register.**
6) **Within moments your course will open, and you can begin studying online.**

NOTES

RESOURCES

Made in the USA
Middletown, DE
06 July 2021